The Complete Ukulele Player

To acces audio visit:
www.halleonardmgb.com/mylibrary

4983-1584-0503-4082

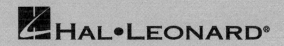

Published by
HAL LEONARD

Exclusive Distributors:
HAL LEONARD
7777 West Bluemound Road,
Milwaukee, WI 53213
Email: info@halleonard.com

HAL LEONARD EUROPE LIMITED
42 Wigmore Street,
Marylebone, London, W1U 2RY
Email: info@halleonardeurope.com

HAL LEONARD AUSTRALIA PTY. LTD.
4 Lentara Court,
Cheltenham, Victoria, 3192 Australia
Email: info@halleonard.com.au

Order No. AM1009624
ISBN 978-1-78305-739-9
This book © Copyright 2015 Hal Leonard

Written by David Harrison.
Edited by Adrian Hopkins.
Cover and prelims designed by Michael Bell Design.
Text pages designed by David Harrison.
Photographs by Matthew Ward Photography.
Music recorded by David Harrison.
Audio mixed and mastered by Jonas Persson.
Printed in the EU.

www.halleonard.com

David Harrison
@dalstondavid
@CompleteUke

Until a few years ago, most people seeing a ukulele would think maybe of George Formby or Hawaii. Recently, though, the uke has enjoyed a huge surge in popularity. The Ukulele Orchestra of Great Britain, which was founded in 1985, did a great deal to change perceptions of the uke but continued to exploit the novelty side of the instrument. However, lots of people are starting to take the uke seriously. It has now usurped the recorder as the instrument of choice in the classroom, and uke groups are starting up all over the place. Record numbers of people are learning and suddenly there are lots of tutor books, songbooks and videos to help you learn. Walk into any music shop these days and you'll see a brightly lit, candy-coloured selection of ukes proudly displayed.

When I was asked to write this book I spent a while talking to teachers and players, beginners, performers and uke fans, to get a better idea of what it is that people love about the uke – and what people seem to want to get out of it. There are lots of different answers, of course, but mainly people tell me they like it because it's quirky, and cheap, and easy to play, and cute; that they like the sound, they like the portability, and they like coming together with others to play. Loads of people like the way songs sound on the uke – rock songs, reggae songs, ballads… songs that were never meant to be uke songs are getting the uke treatment and taking on a whole new life.

One thing's for certain: the ukulele is very easy to learn. Get stuck in to the first few chapters of this book and pick up a handful of chord shapes and you'll be strumming along before you know it.

I've taught people to play musical instruments for over 30 years, and in that time I've picked up some handy tips myself. One of the most useful pieces of advice I can pass on to you is that you should play every single day. Make a space in your day that's just for you and your uke, somewhere quiet and out-of-the-way. Even if you can only manage ten minutes, as long as it's time focused on your practice, and you concentrate on the task at hand, you'll definitely see progress. Be sure to have a specific target for your practice every time you sit down, and take the time to enjoy all your hard work by just playing for the sheer fun of it when your practice is done.

The other tip I have is this: find other people to play with. Other uke players of the same standard; or more advanced players; or guitarists, keyboard players, singers… anyone you can join in with. There's nothing like the feeling of playing music together with other people. It'll bring you huge joy and – when you've been at it for a little while – you'll find other people really like it too.

Take a deep breath. This could turn out to be one of the greatest journeys of all. Good luck!

Before We Start

Introduction

Congratulations on deciding to learn the ukulele—and on buying this book!

If you've played a musical instrument before, you'll find that lots of the terms and ideas here are already familiar to you, and if you haven't, you'll be on your way before you know it.

Why play the ukulele anyway?

Good question! The fact is, the uke is really *easy to learn* and very *easy to play*. There's plenty of fancy stuff you can do on the uke too, but making a simple sound with a few basic chord shapes is extremely straightforward—it's one of those instruments that lets you sound like you know what you're doing right from the beginning.

As you might already know, ukuleles are *not expensive*. You can spend a lot of money on a professional-level instrument, but even these are much cheaper than an equivalent-quality guitar, for instance. The ukulele is also ideal to *play together* with other people. If you have friends who play guitar, you can read the chord names from their music and play them on the uke too.

One more thing to know: the uke is very versatile. If you're into pop, rock, bossa nova, reggae, folk or jazz, you'll find the ukulele lends itself very nicely. We'll look at a variety of styles in this book and explore some tips and tricks to give your playing that authentic edge.

Using the audio

This book is accompanied by a comprehensive set of professionally recorded demonstrations and backing tracks that you can download and keep.

For every song there are two tracks: a demonstration and a backing track.

Whenever you see the audio symbol shown here, be sure to take a listen to the examples to hear exactly what it ought to sound like.

Then try it on your own until you've got the hang of it before finally playing along with the audio.

Unless otherwise shown, all the strumming and picking examples are played using a simple C chord shape (page 18).

How to use this book

This book is designed to be followed, cover-to-cover, to give you all the skills you'll need to play the uke to a decent standard.

Listen to the audio examples and go over all the exercises, and bit by bit things will fall into place. As soon as you've got a few chords under your fingers, you'll find lots of other songs that you can play. There are loads of songbooks available, and some are especially aimed at players with a limited number of chords in their repertoire.

Practice makes perfect

Of course, everyone's different, and the amount of time it takes you to work through the various chapters will depend on how much time and effort you can afford to spend. The single biggest thing that will make an impact is practice.

Get used to playing every day. Play little and often, to avoid burnout, and be sure to set yourself a specific target for each session—maybe playing a new chord cleanly, or making a strumming pattern smoother, or learning a section of a song—so that you know the time you're spending is put to good use.

Some people keep a practice diary to keep tabs on their progress. Whatever you do, don't be tempted to compete with someone else's progress. It's really important to take the time *you* need to absorb the material properly.

Spend some time looking over the guidelines on page 16, which will help give you a good overall posture and technique. Take care to sit comfortably and upright to give yourself the best possible chance of focusing on the uke and avoiding backache or other niggles down the line.

You'll also want some peace and quiet, good lighting, and somewhere to prop your books up where you can see them without hunching—a music stand is ideal for this.

A Little History

How the ukulele came to be

What does *ukulele* mean?

It's well known that the ukulele comes from Hawaii, and its fame and popularity have now spread to make it a world-wide phenomenon.

Its origins can be traced back to the arrival of the *Ravenscrag*, an iron-hulled clipper that brought Portuguese immigrants to Hawaii in 1879. Sailing on a four-month voyage from Madeira to Honolulu, the *Ravenscrag* was among the first ships to bring waves of Portuguese immigrant workers to Hawaii to work on sugar cane plantations.

There are various explanations of the name *ukulele*, which translates roughly as 'jumping flea': according to some sources, a passenger on the *Ravenscrag* named João Fernandes entertained locals playing folk songs from Madeira on a small stringed instrument he had brought with him. His fast-moving fingers were said to resemble jumping fleas.

Another story involves an Englishman named Edward Purvis, Assistant Chamberlain to the last reigning king of Hawaii, King David Kalakaua. Purvis' small frame and energetic demeanour while playing his instrument are said to have earned him—and his instrument—the epithet of *ukulele*.

A further explanation, from the last Hawaiian monarch, Queen Lili'uokalani, is that *ukulele* actually means 'the gift that came here'.

We may never know for certain how the instrument got its name, but it's agreed that the uke grew out of a number of similar stringed instruments that arrived in Hawaii in the 19th century with waves of Portuguese settlers—instruments themselves descended from the lute, the guitar and various folk instruments such as the Madeiran *machete de braça* and the *cavaquinho*, either of which might have been what Fernandes played.

The uke as a distinct instrument was first built by three Madeiran cabinet makers who also arrived on the *Ravenscrag*: Manuel Nunes, José do Espírito Santo, and Augusto Dias. Having finished their contracts on the plantations, all three eventually established themselves as instrument makers, producing *machetes* of various types with local materials. These were the first true ukuleles.

The ukulele was an instant hit in Hawaii. King David Kalakaua himself promoted the new instrument as a native Hawaiian item, featuring it at official functions playing traditional Hawaiian music.

Re-entrant Tuning

One important point: almost every other stringed instrument, such as the guitar, banjo, violin, mandolin, harp, cello... has strings arranged in order of pitch, from low to high in sequence.

The tuning of the ukulele, however, grew out of a variant of *machete* tuning, and has strings out of sequence. It's actually an important factor in the sound of the uke. It's known as **re-entrant** tuning.

So when you're tuning, bear in mind that the third string is the lowest-pitched of all.

The ukulele conquers the world

Various attempts were made to introduce the new instrument to a wider audience, but it wasn't until the Panama Pacific International Exposition at San Francisco in 1915 that it began to make an impression. A growth in popularity on the American mainland of both the uke and the Hawaiian music with which it was associated continued throughout the 1920s.

The simplicity of the ukulele, its portability and relatively inexpensive price made it the perfect instrument for hobby musicians to learn and for singers to accompany themselves. At the height of the uke craze, nearly half of the Martin Guitar company's output was ukuleles, producing around 15,000 instruments in 1925 alone. Sheet music of popular songs routinely included uke chord boxes (*above*).

The ukulele survives

The rise of rock 'n' roll and the electric guitar sidelined the uke, although it remained in the public consciousness through British entertainer George Formby (who played a hybrid *banjolele*) and was later championed by Formby fans including George Harrison.

The uke remained popular in Japan, too, having been a second home to Hawaiian music since its introduction in the 1920s.

The ukulele rises again

The ukulele has been used in the classroom since the late 1960s when Canadian educator, J. Chalmers Doane, introduced the uke as the ideal accessible ensemble instrument, and the advent of the internet allowed instant sharing of technique, tips and tablature.

Today, outfits such as the Ukulele Orchestra of Great Britain and virtuoso players like Jake Shimabukuro have reinvented the uke.

It has replaced the recorder as the most popular school instrument, and artists such as Jason Mraz, Taylor Swift, Bruno Mars and Pearl Jam's Eddie Vedder are frequently seen and heard playing the ukulele.

(Right) Martin Style 1 soprano ukulele, of the type produced on the US mainland in huge numbers at the height of the ukulele boom. Such vintage models now change hands for considerable sums.

Choosing a Ukulele

What to look out for, and what to avoid

The ukulele is a very simple instrument, with four nylon strings stretched over a hollow box along a flat fingerboard divided up into frets. There's not a lot that can go wrong, right?

There's a uke for every budget, from children's instruments that are little more than toys, through beginner instruments that cover the basics, to high-end, hand-crafted ukes that go for the price of a small car! So which one's right for you?

What makes a good uke good?

The very cheapest mass-produced instruments look like a uke and maybe even sound a bit like a uke, but you won't go too far down the road before you discover inaccuracies in the fret spacings and perhaps the angle of the neck; or the position of the bridge; and maybe the feel of the thing. Once you've played for a while you'll realise there's something lacking in the sound— maybe just none of the mellifluous richness that drew you to the uke in the first place.

It stands to reason that the cheapest instruments are produced to sell, rather than play. But you don't have to move much further up the price range to find an instrument that will satisfy your needs.

Solid, resonant tone-woods make a huge difference to the sound, and good-quality hardwood for the fretboard will have a big effect on the feel of the instrument. Check the quality of any mother-of-pearl inlays such as fret markers or the rosette—it'll indicate the overall production quality of the instrument.

If you don't care too much for fancy inlays and other decorations, then take a look at the quality of the finish to the wood, the smoothness of the tuning pegs and the crispness of the shape of the headstock.

The most important thing, of course, is the sound. But since you don't yet play the uke, that's difficult to judge. If you can take a uke player with you when you go shopping, you stand a much better chance of finding a uke that 'speaks' to you.

A top tip: buy at a specialist uke dealer. Lots of music shops have a few ukes, but the extra information and guidance a specialist can supply is priceless. They'll have a wider range of instruments to choose from, too, and there's no reason to worry that you'd be paying more for your instrument than if you bought in a general music store or online. It's a win-win.

How much does a ukulele cost?

You might have a set budget, or you might be prepared to pay whatever it takes to find the perfect instrument. But since you're starting out on the uke, you only really need to spend enough to avoid buying a piece of landfill. Take the time to ask someone you trust about ukes available and be prepared to put in a bit of research so you don't spend too much—or too little on your ukulele.

There are different sizes of uke. The commonest, and the one most suitable for a beginner, is the *soprano*.

By the way, if you're *left handed*, simply reverse the uke—and the strings and tuning. There's no such thing as a left-handed uke, since they're entirely symmetrical.

So I bought a uke. Now what?

Did you buy a case? You'll need a case. Cheaper ukes often come supplied with flimsy carry bags, but to take care of your instrument you'll need either a good quality padded soft case, or—if you're planning to travel—a hard case. Apart from protecting your instrument, a case is a great place to store all your accessories, such as your tuner, spare strings and your music.

Make sure your case fits your instrument snugly. You shouldn't have to ram the uke in, but neither should it rattle around inside.

Whichever instrument you plump for, it might be worth taking it to a luthier for a quick check. For a reasonable fee, he can verify the alignment of everything and give it a tweak here and there if necessary. It can hugely improve the handling and sound of a new instrument.

Trading up

Once you've been playing a while—say six months or a year—you'll have a much better feel for what it is you're looking for in a uke, and a much better idea of whether you're likely to stick with it, so you can always move up to something a bit more fancy in time.

Many advanced uke players buy second-hand instruments. You invariably get more 'bang for your buck' with a used instrument, and it's sometimes possible to make huge savings compared to a brand new ukulele.

Vintage ukes are a specialist market though—and a minefield. Old doesn't necessarily mean great: there are plenty of cheaply-made ukes that have survived 20 or 30 years, and now they're old, but still cheaply-made. Well-made instruments, on the other hand, will certainly improve with age as the tone-woods 'open up' and the true sound of the uke is revealed.

Parts of the Ukulele

What you need to know

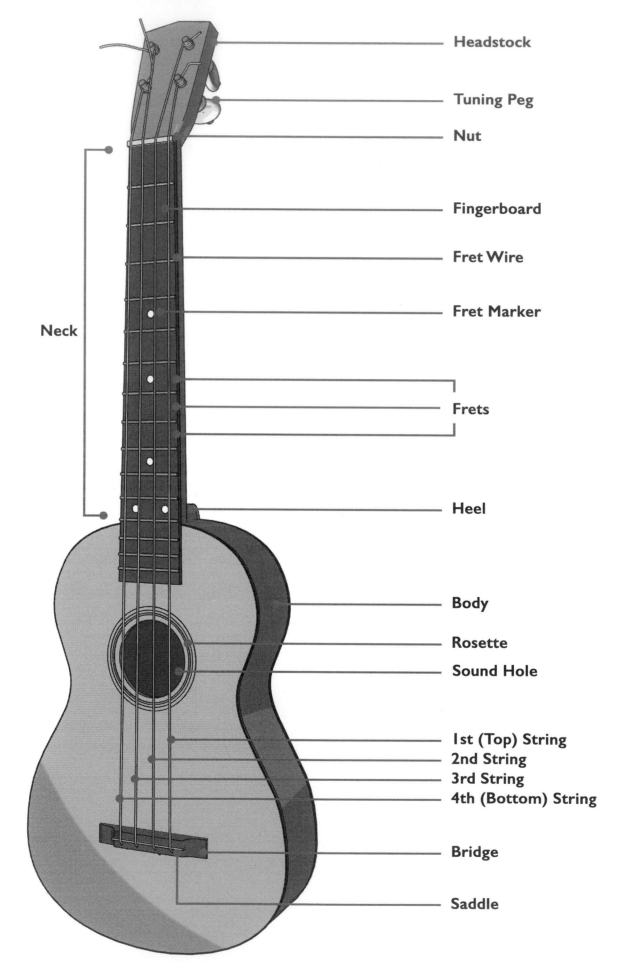

Headstock

Tuning Peg

Nut

Fingerboard

Fret Wire

Fret Marker

Frets

Neck

Heel

Body

Rosette

Sound Hole

1st (Top) String
2nd String
3rd String
4th (Bottom) String

Bridge

Saddle

Accessories

Other things you'll need

The single most important piece of kit after the uke itself is undoubtedly a case. A hard case like the one pictured below will give you plenty of protection but might be cumbersome. A good quality padded one could be a better bet.

Tuning the uke is made a lot easier with an electronic tuner (*above*) and a spare set of strings (*right*) will ensure you're catered for should one snap.

Broken strings aren't often an issue for uke players, but strings do get tired, so get into the habit of replacing them with a new set when you notice a loss of brightness in the sound.

Tuning Up

Getting the strings to sound just right

Getting the strings of the ukulele in tune is essential for a musical sound. Nowadays, with electronic tuners that tell you when the strings are in tune, there's no excuse for having an out-of-tune instrument.

Tuning terms

Before we get started, there are a few important terms to cover:

- *Pitch* refers to how high the sound is. Birdsong is usually high-pitched, and the rumble of traffic is more low-pitched. In music, when we discuss tuning, we talk about the pitch of a note—or the pitch of a string—to mean how high or low it is.

- When a string plays a note that is too high, it's said to be *sharp*. Sharp simply means 'raised pitch'.

- Likewise, a note that's too low is said to be *flat*. Flat just means 'lowered pitch'.

Tuning notes

This illustration shows the names of the strings and the audio tracks.
Before you tune, take a good look at the tuning

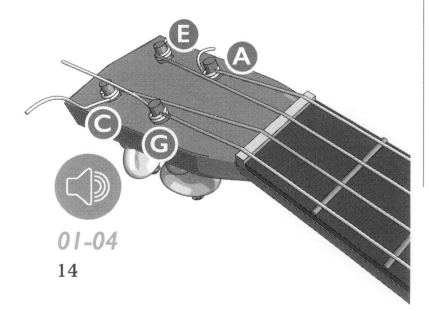

01-04

mechanism on your uke. It'll either be a simple peg that goes through the headstock, or it'll be a geared peg, guitar style, that comes out of the side of the headstock. They both work in the same way.

Tighten the string to make it sharper, or loosen it to make it flatter. Pluck a string with your right-hand thumb and, while the sound is still ringing, turn the corresponding peg. You should hear the note flatten or sharpen, depending on the direction the peg is turned.

Get used to the turning direction, and familiarise yourself with the order the pegs are in—they're in the same sequence on almost any ukulele. Tuning can be a bit fiddly, and it's easy to select the wrong peg by mistake. Strings can get broken that way!

Tuning Methods

Tuning from a sound source

If you want to tune from another sound such as pitch pipes or some recorded audio, it pays to put in a bit of practice. To get used to hearing whether your string is sharp or flat compared with the tuning note, you could try singing both notes—even if you're not a strong singer, you'll instinctively hear whether you're singing higher or lower to match the string.

Start by tuning the C string. Listen carefully to the reference note and pick the C string (third string) with your right-hand thumb. Once you're happy with it, you can use the C string to tune the others.

Here's the plan: place a finger on the 4th fret of the C string, which creates an E. Play it firmly, letting it ring, and compare it to the 2nd string, which should also be an E. You should be able to pick the 3rd and 2nd strings alternately, comparing the sound and operating the 2nd string tuning peg, until the 2nd string matches the 3rd.

Now for the 4th string, which is tuned to G. You can find G by playing a note at the 3rd fret of the 2nd string. As before, alternate

between the reference sound (now on the 2nd string) and the target note (now the 4th) until they match. Remember, the 2nd string is already in tune, so you only want to adjust the pitch of the 4th string.

Finally, you can tune the 1st string, which should be an A. The easiest place to find A is on the 2nd fret of the 4th string. Repeat the process as for the other strings, being sure only to tune the top (1st) string this time. Use the diagram (*below*) to guide you.

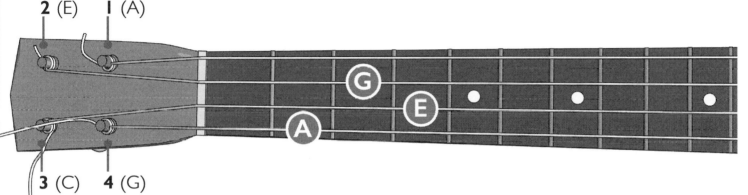

2 (E) **I** (A)

3 (C) **4** (G)

Using a Tuner

Electronic tuners clamp onto the headstock. They 'listen' to the pitch of the strings either through vibrations that travel through the headstock or by means of a built-in microphone. Your tuner might well have a switch to select either option. While there are plenty of different models, they all work the same way. Select the note for the string you want to tune, and the tuner will indicate whether the sound is too flat or too sharp, until you have it perfectly in tune.

Electronic tuners are very accurate and can save a huge amount of time, and they have the added benefit that you can use them to tune your uke even if you can't really hear what's going on, such as in a classroom or on a gig. They are an excellent investment.

Getting Started
Good posture

The uke is famous as a go-anywhere, play-anyhow instrument. But you'll find that spending a moment thinking about how to hold it and how to sit (or stand) will avoid discomfort. Bad posture and technique can lead to muscle strain, cramps and aching shoulders and back.

Standing

Try to maintain a good balance, with both feet firmly on the ground. That way, you'll keep a straight back and the shoulders can relax.

The ukulele is a very light instrument, and can easily be held by gently hugging the body against your ribs or belly with the right forearm. It should stay in position without the need to grip it with the left hand.

A useful tip: keep a music stand at a sensible height so you can easily see your music books wthout hunching or stooping.

Sitting

Be sure to find a seat without arms that lets you sit with a straight back. A stool with a slightly higher—or adjustable—seat is much better than a standard chair. Sitting at the front of a raised seat will help you to hold a relaxed and open posture. Hold the uke against your torso as for the standing position.

Avoid armchairs, sofas and low seats, as you'll end up with back pain after a very short while.

Left hand

For the beginner, it can be tempting to grip the neck of the uke tightly with the left hand. In fact (*right*) the right forearm should provide all the support you'll need. The left hand is there to fret the strings, and the fingers need to be free to move about.

Place the thumb gently at the back of the neck so the fingers can come around to the front in a natural curve (*right*).

The fingertips should be able to press down on the strings with almost no effort. If your thumb is wrapped around the top of the neck too much, you'll limit the amount of free movement that the fingers have.

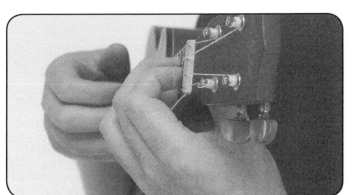

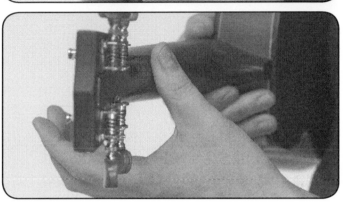

Right hand

The sound is created with the right hand, and we'll spend a fair bit of time looking at strumming technique. But for now, with the right forearm gently cradling the body of the uke, the right hand should be free to move down and up across the strings.

The strumming motion comes largely from the wrist, so it's important to stay relaxed, with a gently curved hand (*left*).

Finger numbers

For the left hand (and occasionally for the right hand), the fingers are numbered. This is very useful for chord shapes, where numbers are used to signify the different fingers. The index finger is 1, the middle finger 2, the ring finger 3 and the little finger 4 (*right*).

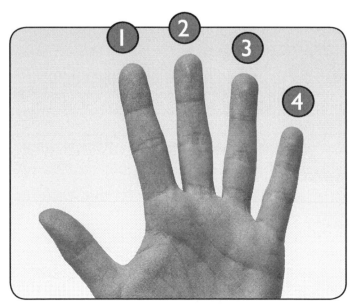

Hand Positions

First Chords

Basic shapes

What is a chord?

A chord is simply a collection of notes played at the same time. We rely on the effect these different notes have on each other to create the character of the chord. On the ukulele, almost everything we do involves chords, since we're generally playing all four strings at once.

Reading chord diagrams

Before we play chord shapes, let's take a look at the way these chords are shown (*right*).

We use **chord boxes**, or chord diagrams, to show where the fingers go. Chords are shown with the neck held vertically. The nut is at the top, with the four strings running down the diagram. The frets are shown as horizontal divisions. Above the strings, optional symbols show that a string is played 'open' (o), meaning it's not fretted, or else the string isn't played (x). Fingers are placed according to large dots. Our diagrams also include numbers, 1-4, corresponding to different finger numbers.

In the music, chord diagrams are simplified graphics like the one here (*right*). Compare it to the large diagram and you'll see that they show exactly the same thing.

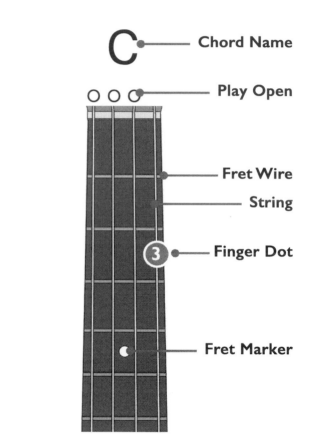

Finger positions

Here's a checklist for fretting chords, creating a clear, musical sound:

- Bring the fingertip onto the string perpendicular to the fingerboard;

- Ensure the finger is touching only the string it's aiming for, leaving the other strings to vibrate freely;

- Position the fingertip just behind the fret wire if possible—this will allow you to fret the string with less effort and should result in a cleaner sound.

C chord

Our first chord is called C. It's one of the most useful chords on the uke, and it's very simple to play. As you can see from the diagram, your third finger should be placed on the 3rd fret of the 1st string, with the other three strings played open (*right*).

Try to ensure that the finger comes down neatly onto the 1st string without touching any of the other strings. When you're ready, brush across the strings with the right-hand thumb to hear how it sounds.

F chord

For the next chord, F, we need two fingers combined. We're adding the first finger on the 1st fret of the 2nd string, together with the second finger on the 2nd fret of the 4th string (*right*). The 1st and 3rd strings are played open.

Strum across the strings to hear how it sounds, and tweak your left-hand finger positions if the strings don't all sound clearly.

G⁷ chord

The final chord we'll look at for now is called G^7. It requires three fingers. This time, keep the first finger in the same position as for the F chord—at the 1st fret of the 2nd string— and swing the 2nd and 3rd strings into place at the 2nd fret of the 3rd and 1st strings.

Notice the triangular shape the finger dots make: this will help you to visualise the chord in future.

First Chords

Blowin' In The Wind

Bob Dylan

Bob Dylan's 'Blowin' in the Wind' became an acoustic anthem for the 1960s protestors who cast the young folk singer as their revolutionary troubadour. It was not a role that Dylan relished and in 1965 he embarked on a career of regular self-reinvention with his controversial introduction of electric rock numbers to the Newport Folk Festival.

Let's put the new chord shapes into practice with one of the most popular of all three-chord songs.

Changing chords

It's very useful to learn to change from one chord shape to another. Think about what the shapes have in common, and how they are different. For instance, how would you transition from C to F? And from F to G^7? Try going backwards and forwards between C and F, getting your fingers used to the shapes.

This Dylan classic is played over a four-beat rhythm: play each chord with a single strum down with the thumb across the strings, letting the chord ring on for four beats.

The music is divided into short rhythmic sections called **bars**, separated by **barlines**. In this song, each bar is four beats long. Sections are divided by **double barlines**.

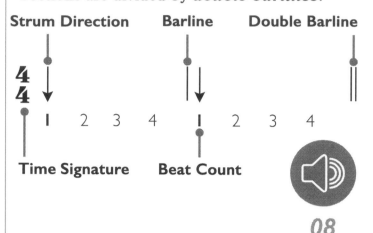

Notice the stacked pair of numbers at the beginning, called the **time signature** (see page 64). The end of the piece is indicated by a thicker barline.

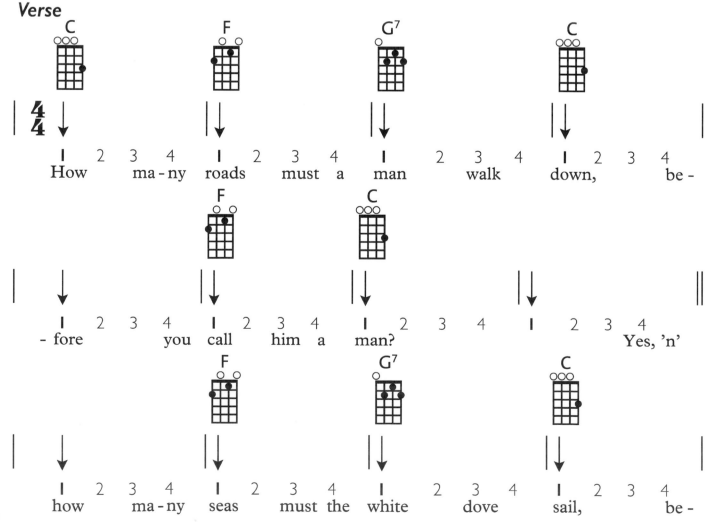

First Chords

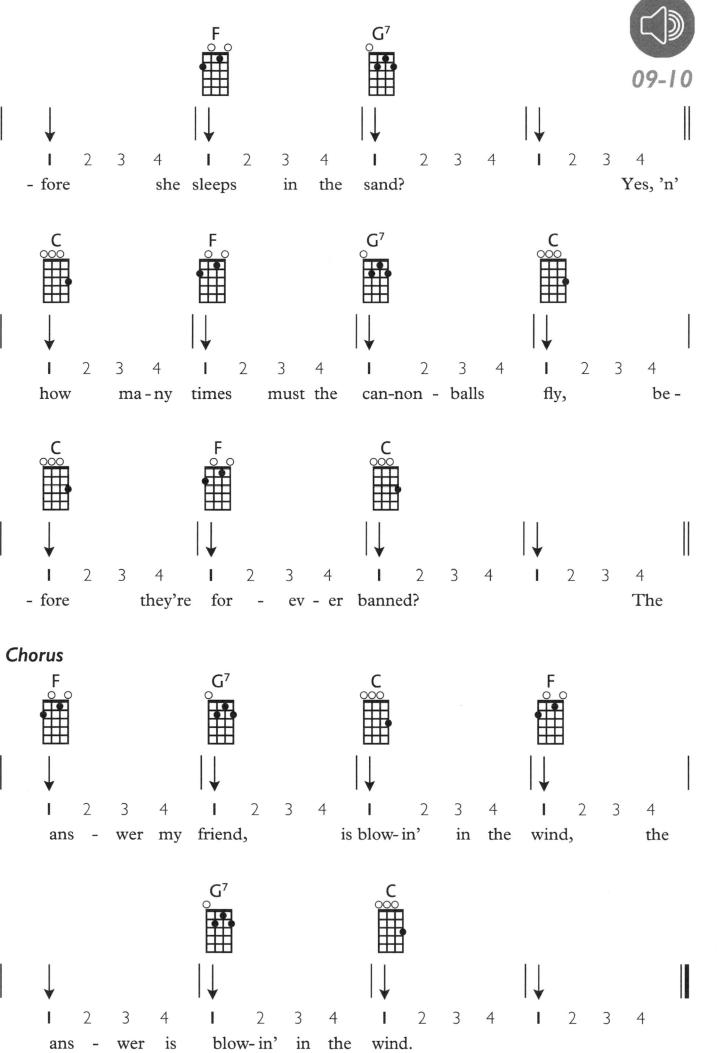

First Chords

- fore   she sleeps   in   the   sand?   Yes, 'n'

how   ma - ny   times   must the   can-non - balls   fly,   be -

- fore   they're   for   -   ev - er   banned?   The

Chorus

ans - wer my   friend,   is blow-in'   in   the   wind,   the

ans - wer is   blow-in'   in   the   wind.

Full chords and lyrics for this song can be found at the back of the book   21

Love Me Do

The Beatles

Written by Lennon & McCartney, 'Love Me Do' was the first single recorded by The Beatles. Released in 1962 it was a simple bluesy number with a distinctive harmonica solo played by Lennon. Catchy and memorable, 'Love Me Do' was a hit but gave little notice of the band's extraordinary melodic and structural invention that would very soon follow.

Let's look at two more simple chord shapes that you'll use again and again: G and D.

First Chords

G chord

You can think of this G chord shape as being like a back-to-front G⁷. Remember the G⁷ triangle? Well now it's pointing the other way!

 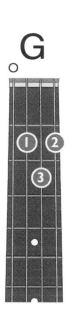

Put the first finger on the 3rd string at the 2nd fret; and the second finger likewise on the 2nd fret, but on the 1st string, and now place the third finger onto the 3rd fret of the 2nd string.

D chord

Now here's a shape that's easy to remember. D (below) uses three fingers all on the same fret. You probably won't be able to get them all right behind the fret wire, but if you check that your thumb is behind the neck rather than wandering around to the front, you'll stand a better chance of getting the fingertips to come down neatly onto the fret.

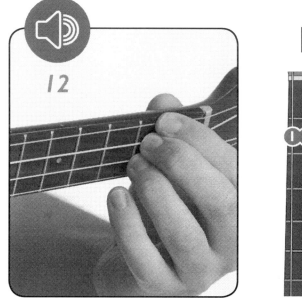 

The verse is played twice. The repeated section is shown by a heavy double barline and a small pair of dots—a **repeat barline**—at the end of the verse (*right*).

Notice the square brackets at the end of the repeated verse—they're **first** and **second time** bars, providing different endings for each repeat (*right*):

By the way, N.C. at the end of the third line simply means 'No chord'—just don't play at that point!

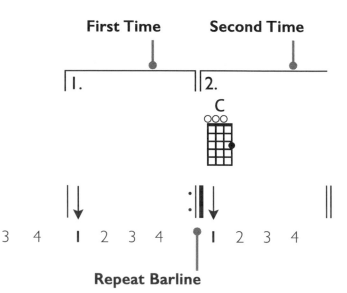

22

Full chords and lyrics for this song can be found at the back of the book

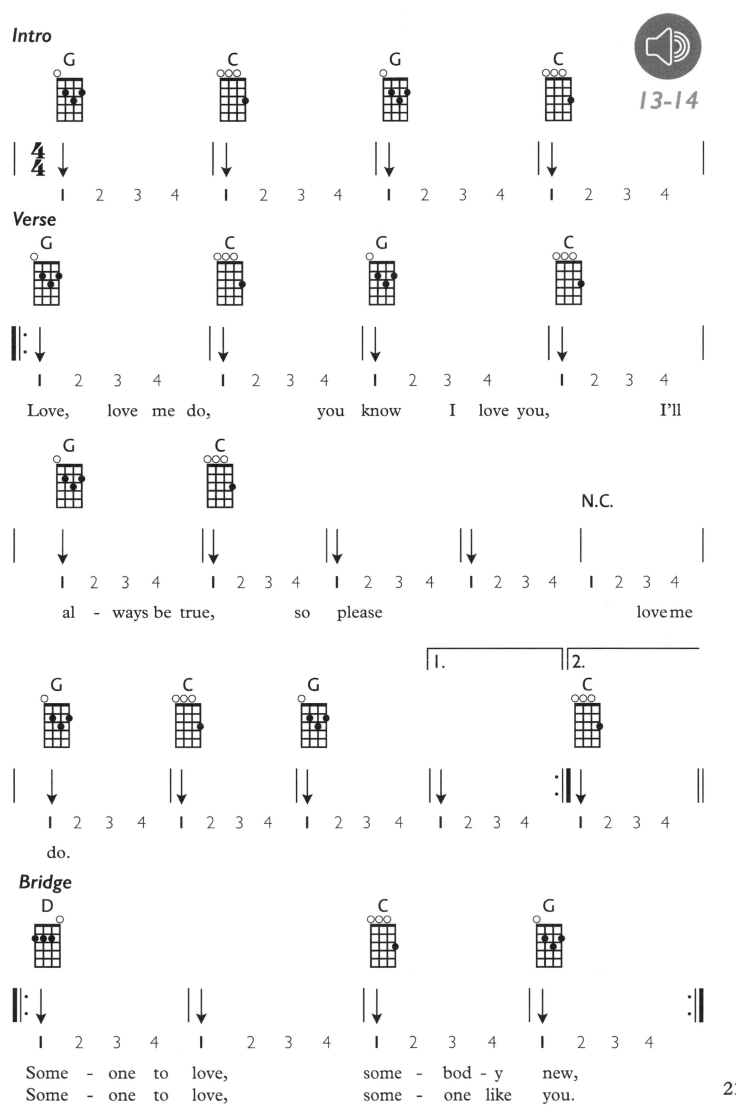

Redemption Song
Bob Marley

Bob Marley's 1980 acoustic recording of one of his most political songs has become a widely-revered track. Channelling the sentiments of the Jamaican political thinker Marcus Garvey who advocated 'freedom of the mind' as a necessary complement to physical freedom, 'Redemption Song' sounds at its most personal in solo acoustic form.

Let's add a couple more chords to our repertoire: Am and Em.

Minor chords

The little m in the chord name stands for *minor*. The sound of these chords might be described as mournful, or dark, or perhaps introverted, compared to the other chords we've played so far. F, C, D and G are all *major* chords, characterised by a bright and cheerful sound.

Chord types

We can use different types of chords to create different moods, and major and minor chords are the most important types.

Am chord

Am, or A minor, is a very straightforward shape, with nothing but a note on the 4th string, 2nd fret, played with the second finger.

Remember G7? That's actually a *major* chord, but with an extra note, the '7'. There's more on that starting on page 56.

Em chord

Em (E minor) is a lot like the G chord shape we looked at for 'Love Me Do'. Now, instead of a note on the 2nd fret of the 3rd string, it's moved up to the 4th fret. You'll need to change the fingering, with the first finger up on the top string.

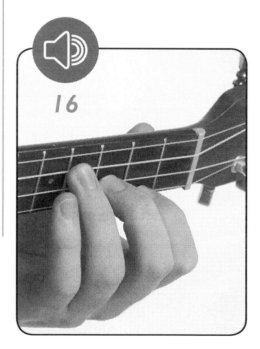

Em

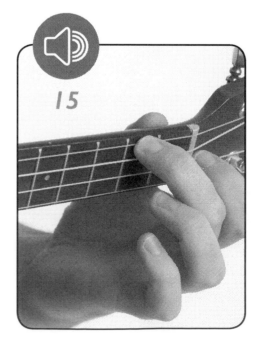

Am

First Chords

Keeping the beat

Up till now, we've concentrated on sounding each chord once at the beginning of the bar. It doesn't really matter whether you brush down across the strings with your thumb or stroke them with your fingers, just as long as you create an even, reliable sound at the start of each bar. The idea is to provide a steady pulse to the music.

When we look at strumming in detail, we'll examine various ways to create a more interesting accompaniment, but we can easily change things a bit to give us something more musical right now: instead of playing the chord once on the first beat of the bar, let's play again on the third beat. It looks like this:

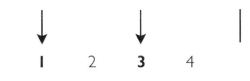

| 1 | 2 | 3 | 4 |

> You'll just need to make sure that you bring the strumming hand back up after the first strum, so it's ready for the next one. This means you'll be strumming down twice in the bar instead of just the once.

In fact, in the chorus of 'Redemption Song' (*overleaf*) you'll notice that sometimes there are actually two different chords in the bar:

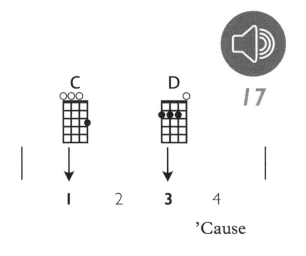

C   D   *17*

| 1 | 2 | 3 | 4 |

'Cause

Now that we're starting to think about rhythms, this is a good time to examine the position of the right hand again.

While the forearm is gently supporting the body of the uke, the right arm should be free to move down and up across the strings. It's worth repeating that the hand movement should come from the wrist.

Try to make your hand movement natural and relaxed, as if you were painting with a big, wet brush!

By the way, this song has an *opening* repeat barline at the start of the second bar, as well as a closing one later on:

Verse

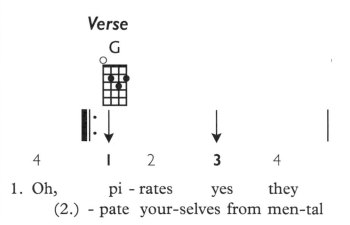

G

| 4 | 1 | 2 | 3 | 4 |

1. Oh,   pi - rates   yes   they
    (2.) - pate   your-selves   from   men-tal

Redemption Song

Bob Marley

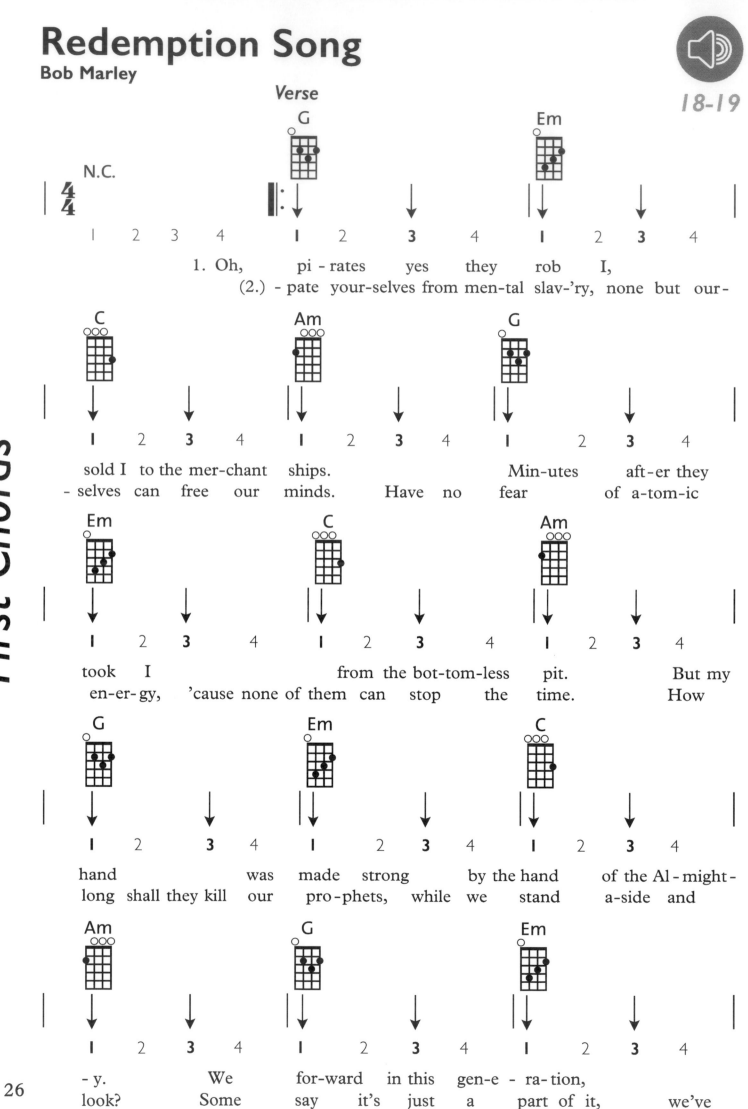

First Chords

Full chords and lyrics for this song can be found at the back of the book

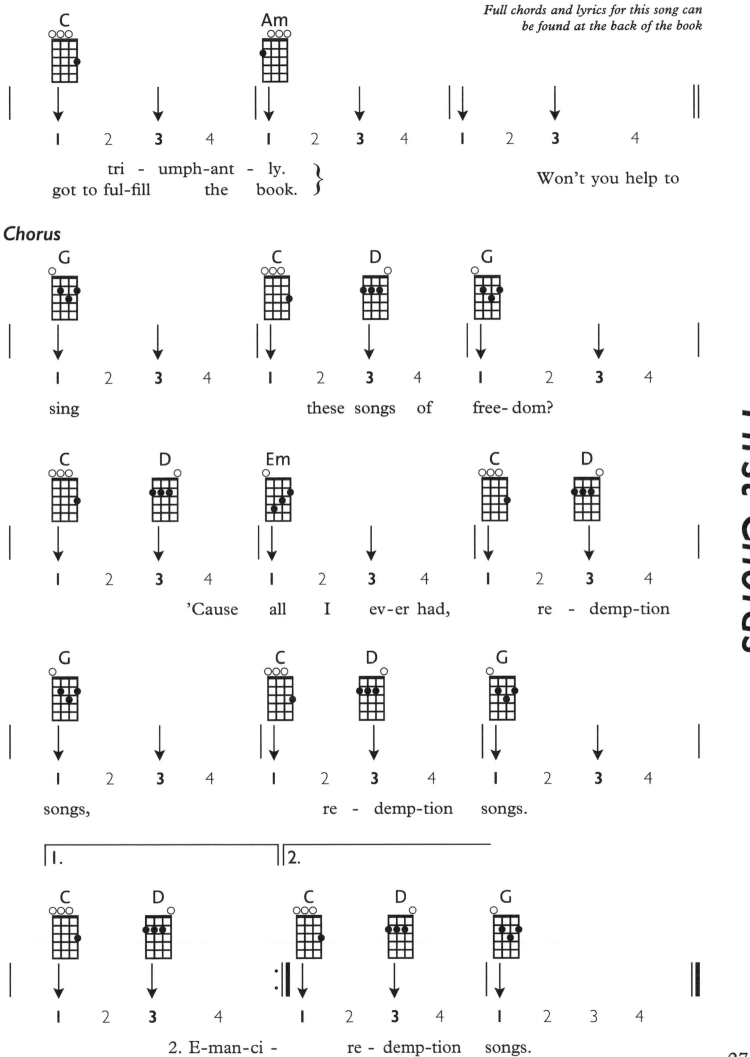

First Chords

27

Strumming Basics
Right-hand rhythm

Now that you've got a few chord shapes under the fingers, it's time to give them some rhythm!

On the uke, the right hand brushes across the strings in time to the beat: this is known as *strumming*.

Strumming options

Most modern instruments have a recognised 'best practice' from a single, unbroken classical tradition. Ukulele strumming techniques have been shaped by many distinct influences, from the classic Spanish folk and flamenco *rasgueado* traditions, to Portuguese *machete*, steel-string acoustic folk styles and the novelty strumming techniques of George Formby's banjolele wizardry.

Uke strumming falls roughly into two camps: firstly, *index finger strumming*, a technique that predominantly uses the index finger strumming across the strings in both directions, and sometimes additionally includes the thumb. This technique was popular on Hawaii when the uke began to take off in the 1920s, and many early tutor books feature this method. This technique is the basis of Formby's style.

Secondly, a *whole-hand strumming* approach, which for example is popular with guitarists who have moved over to the ukulele. In this strumming technique, several fingers are used to strum down across the strings, with the thumb usually providing the upward strums.

The strumming style you choose will be down to what feels natural for your hands. There's no 'right' or 'wrong' way to play, so feel free to pick and choose—and even mix and match elements of both strumming styles.

INDEX FINGER STRUMMING

Down-strum

Holding the right hand loosely over the sound hole, brush down across all four strings with the back of the first finger (*right*).

Be sure to keep the finger relaxed and rotate the wrist to create the movement.

Once you've played one strum, the hand should return to the original position for the next strum. Eventually this will become automatic.

Up-strum

Once you're happy with the down-strum, let's add some up-strums. As you can imagine, this simply means strumming with the finger moving up across the strings instead of down.

In practice, up-strums happen in between down-strums. Think of them as pairs, with the strumming finger moving down-up, down-up, all the time.

As with the down-strum, the movement comes from the wrist. Get used to rotating the wrist gently and think of the finger as a soft brush (*right*).

Go through the checklist below to make sure everything is as it should be.

- Right hand is held loosely in a comfortable, relaxed position.

- The movement comes from the wrist, not from the finger itself.

- All four strings are strummed equally, one after the other.

By the way—and this is a tip for any kind of strumming technique—spend a little while trying out strumming at different points along the strings.

Down towards the bridge you'll produce a brighter, more brittle sound, while further up towards the sound hole the sound is sweeter and warmer. Varying the strumming position is a great way to add different effects to your sound.

WHOLE-HAND STRUMMING

Although many uke purists opt for index finger strumming, it can be hard on the single fingertip—and the nail. Playing with all of the fingers distributes the impact more evenly and allows you to alter the **dynamics** (how loud or soft a strum is) more easily.

Down-strum

Holding the right hand loosely over the sound hole, brush down across all four strings with the back of all four fingers. It's especially important to let the fingertips trail over the strings like a brush—don't try to dig them in.

If you have good strong nails, so much the better, but feel free to experiment with the point of contact for each finger. It will affect the sound.

As with index finger strumming, keep the hand relaxed and create the movement by rotating the wrist.

Once the strum is complete, the hand should be in position, ready for an up-strum...

With this technique in *theory* you'll use all your fingers to strum down, but in *practice* as the tempo increases you'll probably use no more than the first and second fingers, especially at faster tempos. For now, though, just sweep in a relaxed, natural fashion.

Up-strum

The up-strum is played with the back of the thumb.

After a down-strum, the thumb should be in position, a little below the 1st string. Simply bring the hand back up, trailing the thumb across the strings.

As with the down-strum, you'll want to experiment until you have the tip of the thumb just where you want it to create a bright, regular and controlled sound. Listen to the *type* of sound you create—and *how much*.

At the top of the stroke, you should be in position to play another down-strum as before.

Reading the beats

As we've already seen, arrows show the direction of the music, with the beat counts written below. In this example, they're all down-strums (*right*).

Count "*one, two, three, four*" out loud. Try it over and over, aiming for a steady, constant sound. Try it on the other chords you've learnt, too.

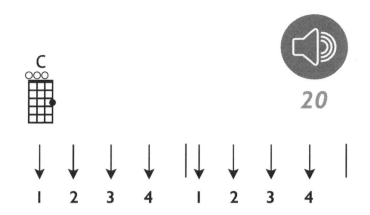

Half-beats

In the example below, the hand strums down on every beat as before, but this time it strums on the way up, too—half-way through each beat.

Notice how the count below the music now says "*one-and-two-and-three-and-four-and*". The '*and*' is the standard way to name the in-between beats.

Be sure to count very steadily, and try to play the up-strums at the same even volume as the down-strums.

Later, we'll add **accents** and other details that will give the strumming a bit more character, but for now it's a good idea to get a solid foundation by ensuring everything is rock steady.

Next, we'll create strumming **patterns** to combine chords into **sequences**.

Stand By Me
Ben E. King

This fine song came about as a hybrid creation between its original singer Ben E. King, and the legendary songwriters Jerry Leiber and Mike Stoller. King's background in church music explains the song's debt to the gospel number 'Lord, Stand By Me', while Leiber & Stoller added distinctive flourishes that helped make it a huge hit. To date it has been recorded by over 400 other artists.

Strumming pattern

Let's put some basic strumming technique into practice, with a simple pattern that uses a combination of down-strums and up-strums.

Start by playing down-up, down-up, in half-beats, as shown on the previous pages. Play steadily and evenly.

Now—keeping the strumming hand moving all the while—strum only where shown: down and up on beats 1 and 3, with perhaps a light strum just before the 3rd beat too:

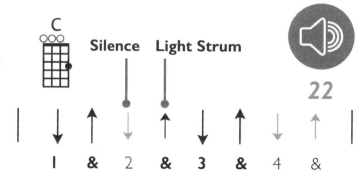

The main thing here is to **keep the hand moving**. The greyed-out arrows show the hand movement—even when the hand isn't strumming. It'll take a bit of practice, but if you take it slowly at first, it'll soon come naturally.

As you pick up the tempo, you'll start to hear a rhythm emerging. Try counting out loud, saying 'mm' in the silences, like this: *"one-and-mm-and-three-and-mm-mm"*.

There's a single new chord shape to learn, too: D⁷. It uses fingers on the 2nd and 4th strings. You could use the second and third fingers, but you might try the first and third fingers instead, since that's what you use for the similar D shape.

Intro

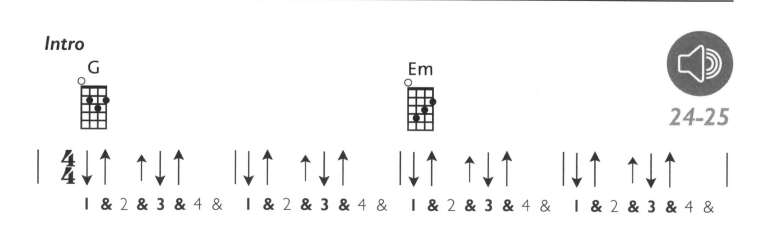

32

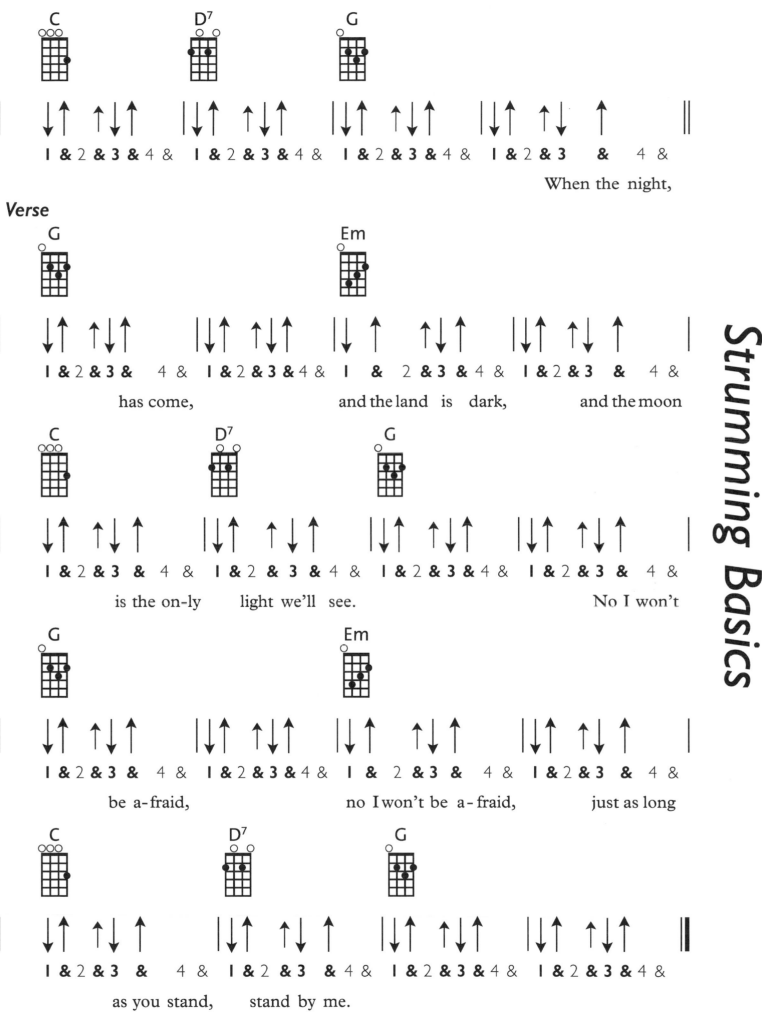

Brown Eyed Girl

Van Morrison

Back in 1967 Van was re-launching his recording career in Northern Ireland after splitting from Decca and his band. The calypso-flavoured 'Brown Eyed Girl' was one of his early songs for the Bang label. Morrison's experiences with Bang were less than happy but the seductive 'Brown Eyed Girl' was a hit and was to become a perennial favourite on classic rock radio.

Recap

Now that things are hopefully starting to come together, let's take a moment to go over a few points again, just to make sure that everything's as it should be:

- Are both hands moving freely, with the right-hand wrist nice and loose, and the left-hand fingertips placed neatly on the fingerboard?

- Is the strumming hand automatically moving down-up, down-up, *even if* it's not always strumming the strings?

New strumming pattern

Here's a really versatile strumming pattern that builds on the work we've just been doing.

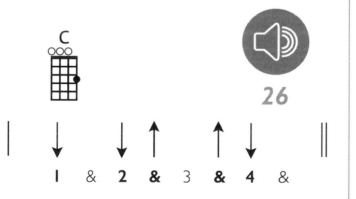

Play a down-strum on the 1st beat; and another on the 2nd beat, this time followed by an up-strum. Finally there's a down-strum on the 4th beat, which is immediately preceded by an up-strum.

Try moving your strumming hand continually down and up without playing as you count *"one-mm-two-and-mm-and-four-mm"*.

Eventually you'll reduce this to *"down, down-up, up-down"* in rhythm.

As always, try it slowly at first, so you can be sure the individual strums are in the correct place—and in the right direction—until you feel ready to start picking up the tempo.

Don't forget to count out loud. If it feels as though it's getting away from you, slow it down again, double-checking the details.

Getting in the habit

Strumming a rhythm like this is a knack. As long as you're having to count out loud and think about each individual strum of the pattern, it'll be difficult to think about changing chords, or singing along.

Eventually, you'll begin to think of the pattern as a single action that you can just keep playing in the background while you get on with focusing on the left hand and the lyrics.

But this all takes time, and different people get to this point in different ways. One thing that everyone can agree on, though, is repetition and focus are the keys to good practice. Put the hours in, and you'll soon be in good shape.

Take a look at the chord sequence for this song. You'll notice that the song begins with a four-bar repeating sequence of G-C-G-D.

Learn this off by heart, and you'll find you don't have to spend the whole time looking at the music while you play, leaving you free to concentrate on strumming and playing the shapes correctly.

Full chords and lyrics for this song can be found at the back of the book

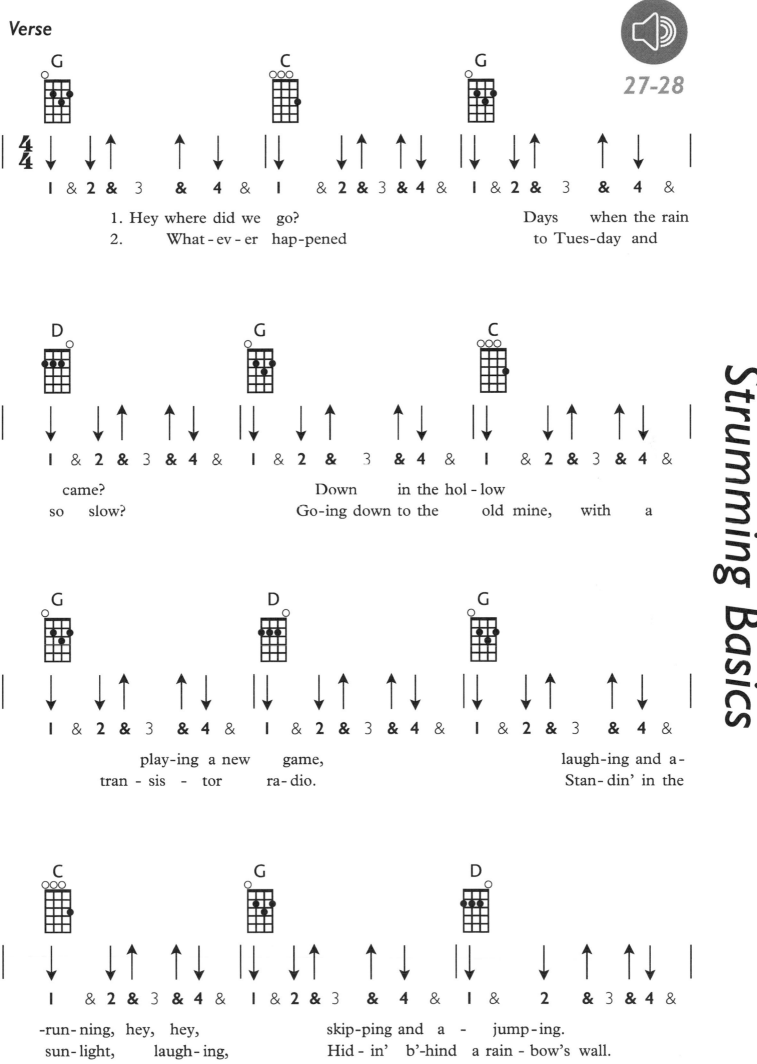

Strumming Basics

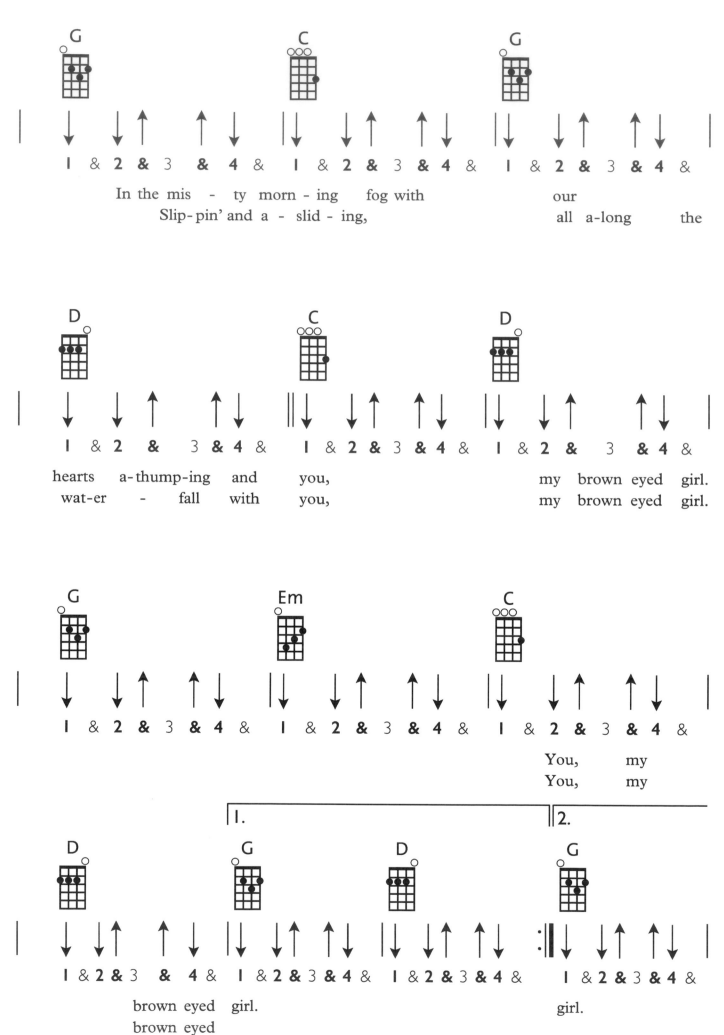

36

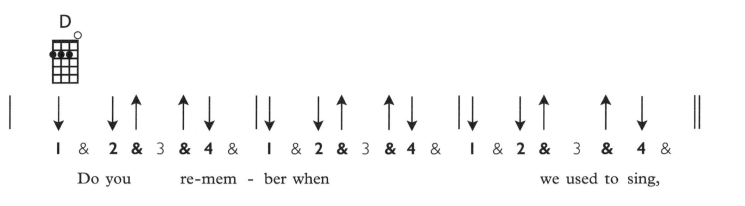

D

| ↓ | ↓ ↑ | ↑ ↓ | | ↓ ↑ | ↑ ↓ | | ↓ ↑ | ↑ ↓ | |

1 & **2** & 3 **& 4** & **1** & **2** & 3 **& 4** & **1** & **2** & 3 **& 4** &

Do you   re-mem - ber when   we used to sing,

Chorus

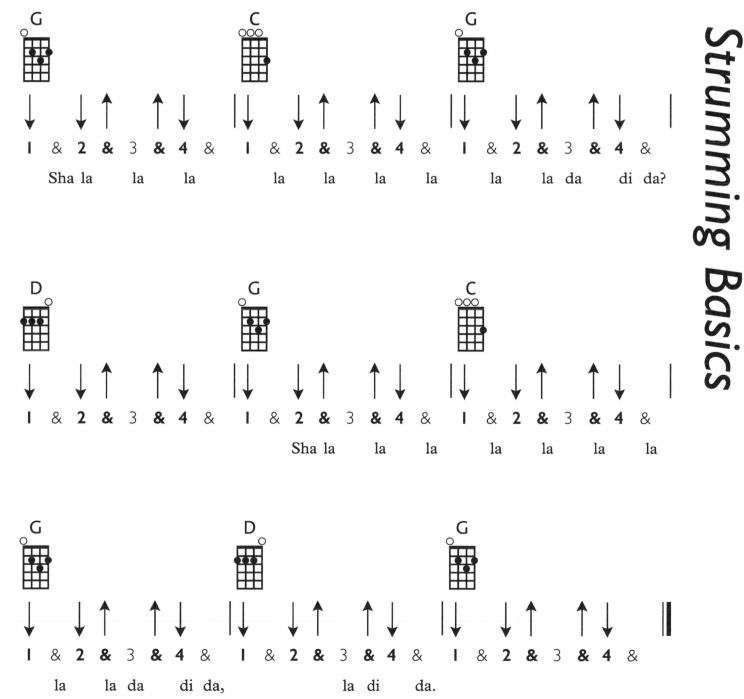

G   **C**   **G**

| ↓ | ↓ ↑ | ↑ ↓ | | ↓ ↑ | ↑ ↓ | | ↓ ↑ | ↑ ↓ | |

1 & **2** & 3 **& 4** & **1** & **2** & 3 **& 4** & **1** & **2** & 3 **& 4** &

Sha la   la   la   la   la   la   la   la   la da   di da?

D   **G**   **C**

| ↓ | ↓ ↑ | ↑ ↓ | | ↓ ↑ | ↑ ↓ | | ↓ ↑ | ↑ ↓ | |

1 & **2** & 3 **& 4** & **1** & **2** & 3 **& 4** & **1** & **2** & 3 **& 4** &

                                Sha la   la   la   la   la   la   la

G   **D**   **G**

| ↓ | ↓ ↑ | ↑ ↓ | | ↓ ↑ | ↑ ↓ | | ↓ ↑ | ↑ ↓ | |

1 & **2** & 3 **& 4** & **1** & **2** & 3 **& 4** & **1** & **2** & 3 **& 4** &

la   la da   di da,   la di   da.

More With Chord Shapes

How to get the most out of basic chords

Which way is up?

It might seem ridiculous, but the words *up* and *down* can mean lots of different things on the ukulele—depending on what you're talking about. Take a look at the diagram below.

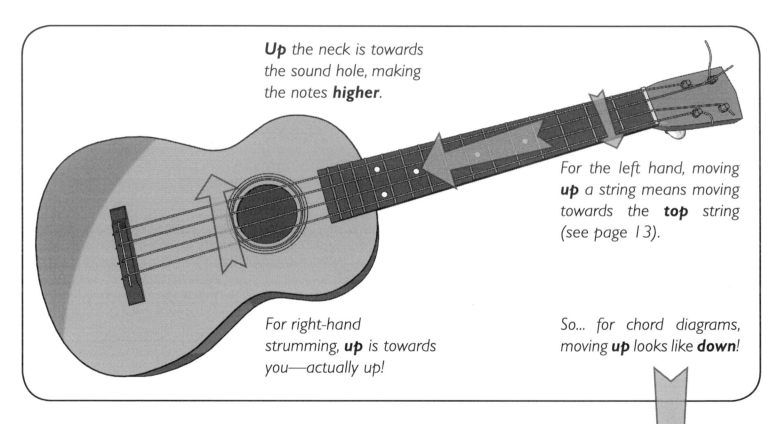

Up the neck is towards the sound hole, making the notes **higher**.

For the left hand, moving *up* a string means moving towards the **top** string (see page 13).

For right-hand strumming, **up** is towards you—actually up!

So... for chord diagrams, moving **up** looks like **down**!

In this section we're going to be talking about moving chord shapes *up the neck*, so 'up' means *towards the sound hole*.

Moving shapes up and down the neck

We'll start with a simple example: F. If we were to move all the notes of this chord up the neck a couple of frets, we should find that we have another major chord (*right*).

Notice that we've moved *all* the notes up two frets, including the notes that were originally on open strings.

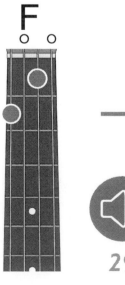

F

29

So how do I play it?

Do you see the curved line above the 2nd fret finger dots (*below*)? This indicates that a single finger frets both notes by laying across the fingerboard. This is known as a **barre**.

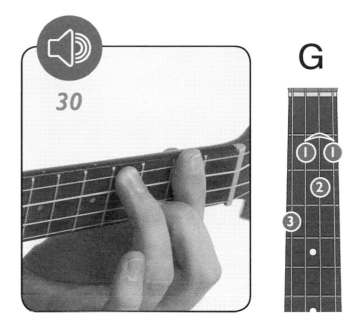

G

As you can see, the first finger lies on the fingerboard at the 2nd fret, parallel to the fret wire, to finger both the 3rd and 1st strings.

Now that all the strings are fretted, the same shape can be used higher up the neck as well. Try moving the shape up as far as you like, checking that the fingers remain in the same relative position. Here it is two frets higher, barred on the 4th fret. Notice the fret number is indicated in the chord diagram (*below*).

A

4fr

Naming chords

Chords (and notes) are named for the first seven letters of the alphabet: A-B-C-D-E-F-G. *Mostly*, these letters are two frets apart. Moving the F chord up two frets creates a chord of G; and moving it two more frets makes a chord of A (*bottom left*).

Compare the G chord (*left*) with the one we first saw on page 22—they're a bit different, but they're both perfectly good G chords.

There are two pairs of notes that are only **one** fret apart: B-C and E-F. With this in mind, try moving the shape up the neck in search of a C chord.

B

6fr

We've already barred this shape on the 4th fret for A, and if we move it up two more frets, barring on the 6th fret, it's a B chord (*right*):

C

7fr

Now we need to move it up just one more fret, to the 7th fret, to create a C chord (*right*).

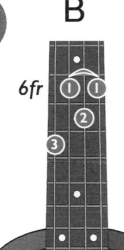

More With Chord Shapes

More barre chords

Let's try some other examples of barred chords using shapes we've already played. We'll start with the plain old C shape we first saw on page 19.

Notice that it has three open strings. When the shape is played higher up the neck, they will need to be covered by a barre.

C

Here's how it looks moved two frets higher, up on the 2nd fret:

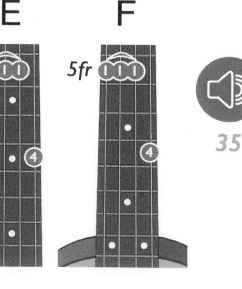

34

D

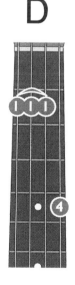

How does the D chord (*left*) compare with the one on page 22?

Can you hear that the new F chord (*below left*) shares a basic sound characteristic with the F shape on page 19?

E   F

As we now know, we can move it up two more frets for E, and just a single fret higher for F:

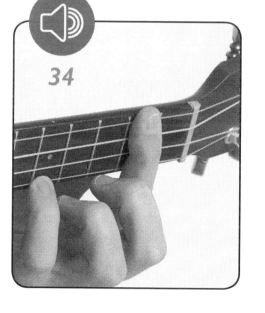

35

While we're at it, there's one more important major chord shape to try. Here's another A chord:

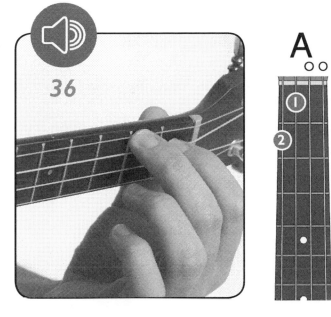

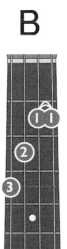

A

Of course, with two open strings, we'll need another barre to handle this shape correctly as we move it up the neck.

Barring on the 2nd fret creates a B chord (*right*)...

37

B

...while up on the 3rd fret it becomes a new C chord. This is a very useful shape.

Compare this C with the one on the previous page.

38

C

Putting barre chords into action

To get to grips with these barre chords, try going back over some of the songs we've looked at, to see if you can replace chord shapes in those songs with new shapes.

For example, for 'Brown Eyed Girl' (page 35) you could try new shapes for G, C and D. Here are the original shapes, with optional barred shapes below:

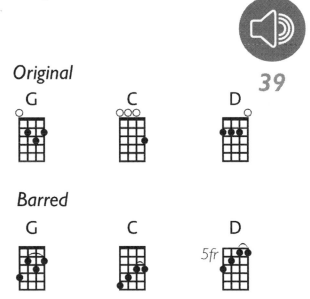

39

Play the song slowly through with these alternative shapes, and you'll begin to see how well they link together. Barre chords can help you find more convenient shapes with less movement from one chord to the next. We'll be seeing more barre chords shortly.

Mull Of Kintyre

Wings

One of the definitive hits of Paul McCartney's post-Beatles Wings outfit, 'Mull Of Kintyre' celebrated the headland of a Scottish peninsula where the ex-Beatle had bought a farm. Written with fellow band member Denny Laine, this rolling, melodic waltz featured stirring bagpipes and its release was cannily timed to ensure massive international sales for Christmas of 1977.

Chord Shape Options

Here's an opportunity to put these barre chords into practice straight away. This simple song has only three chords, all of which can be played with a barre:

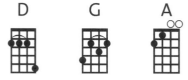

Both G and D are barred at the 2nd fret, while the A is shown played on the 1st and 2nd frets.

Alternatively you could just as easily move the G shape up two frets to play an A chord barred at the 4th fret instead (*right*).

Strumming Pattern

'Mull Of Kintyre' has three beats to the bar—hence the '3' at the top of the time signature—making a classic 'boom-ching-ching' rhythm. Count *"one-and-two-and-three-and"*. The pattern written here has a down-strum on every beat, with the addition of a single up-strum on 'two-and':

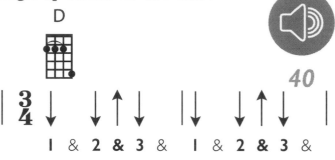

D.C. al Fine

Italian terms help you navigate the music in conjunction with the repeat barline. *Da Capo al Fine* means 'from the beginning to the finish'. *Fine* is at the end of the chorus.

So: play the chorus, then verse 1; return to the chorus and play verse 2. Finally, play the chorus once more to end the song.

Chorus

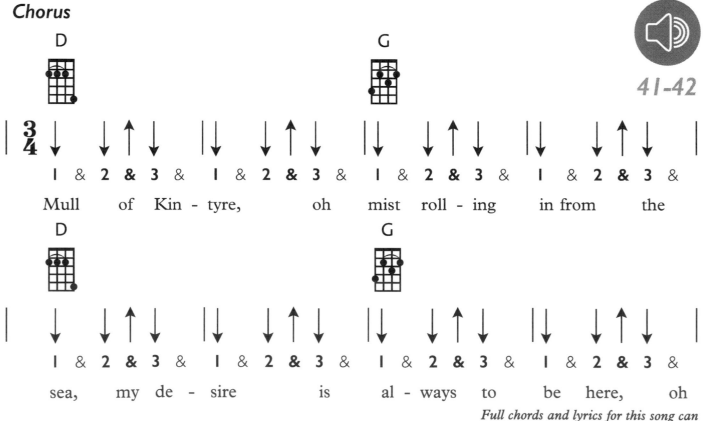

Full chords and lyrics for this song can be found at the back of the book

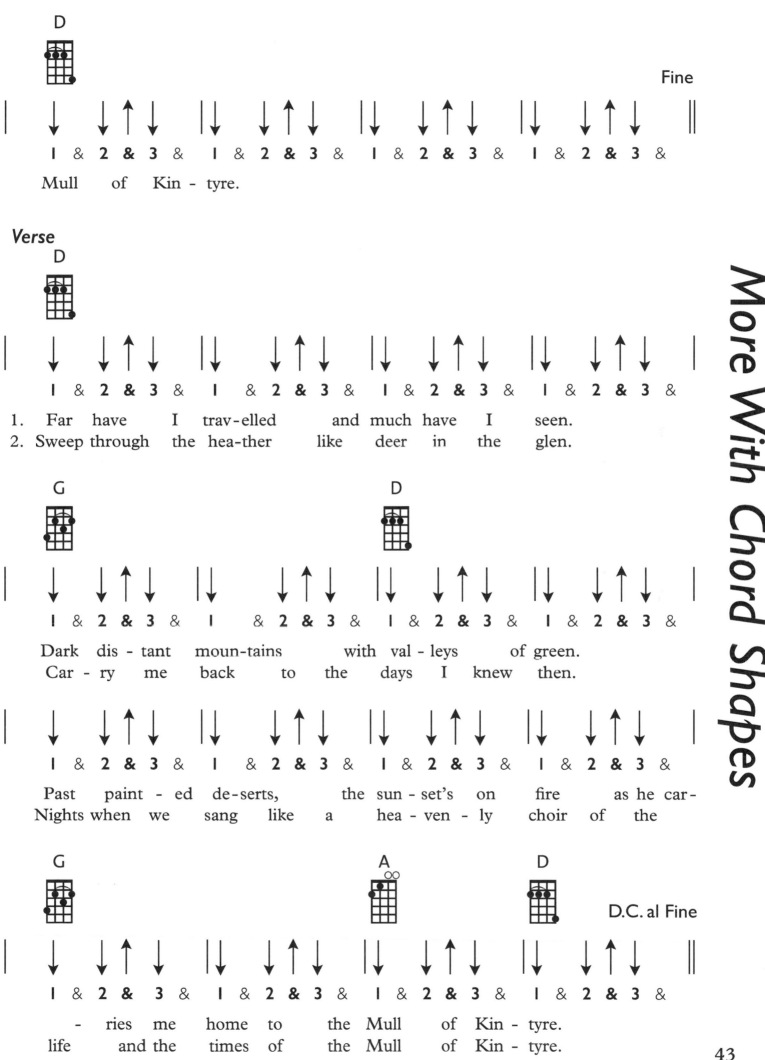

43

Useful minor chord shapes

This simple Am shape from page 24 is easy to barre and move up the neck:

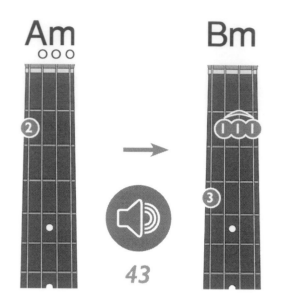

Here's another new minor shape that's very handy. Compare it to the Em shape we used for 'Redemption Song' (page 26):

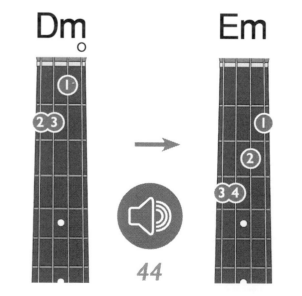

> Of course you can move these shapes up as far as you like: two frets to move between any neighbouring letter names, except between B-C and E-F, which are only one fret apart.

And here's one more minor shape:

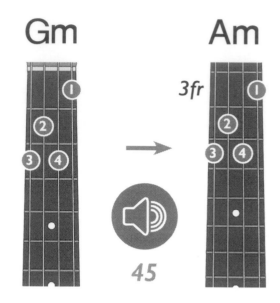

Between them, the three minor chord shapes on this page are almost all you need to play any minor chord.

Eventually, you'll start to develop an intuition about which shape to use. It's very common to play the same chord with more than one shape in the same song.

For example, the two Am shapes on this page might both come in handy in a single piece of music.

Having different shapes for the same chord gives you a range of options to change the overall 'colour' of a chord, and it also means you're likely to find a suitable shape close at hand, regardless of where you are on the neck.

Turn to page 47 and play through 'Ain't No Sunshine' for a good example of this.

Sharps and flats

So far, we've moved up from one note name to the next, two frets at a time—or just one fret to get from B-C and E-F.

But there are in-between chords, too. Take a look at the Bm shape below, and move it down one fret, barring on the 1st fret, like this:

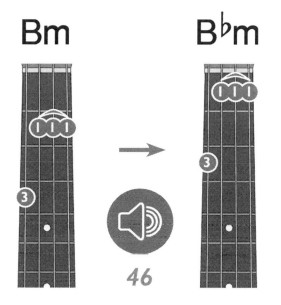

Bm   B♭m

46

So what is this new chord? A chord lowered by a fret is said to be *flattened*, and the ♭ symbol is used. In this case Bm is lowered to become B♭m (spoken as 'B flat minor').

As you know, if this Bm shape were raised one fret it would be Cm. But what about if it were raised again, barred on the 4th fret?

C♯m

4fr

Now it's a Cm chord raised one fret, so it's *sharpened*. We use the ♯ symbol for this. C♯m is pronounced 'C sharp minor'.

Barred at the 5th fret, it would be Dm. So here on the 4th fret you could equally call it D♭m.

47

Seventh chords

To finish up, let's add the two *seventh* (^{7}) shapes we've seen so far, and adapt them to make barre chords, too.

These are major chords with an additional note that gives the chord a particular sound. Seventh chords often sound as though they want to lead on to another chord.

Firstly, here's G^7 from page 19, moved up two frets to make A^7. Notice that the first finger doesn't actually make a barre; it frets just the bottom string.

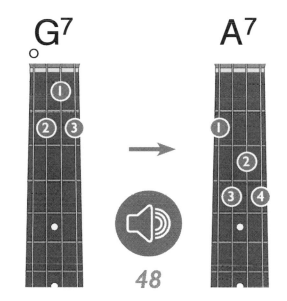

G^7 A^7

48

And now here's D^7 from page 32, moved up two frets and barred on the 2nd fret to make E^7:

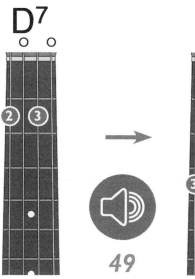

D^7 E^7

49

More With Chord Shapes

Ain't No Sunshine
Bill Withers

Bill Withers was inspired to write this song by a 1962 movie, *The Days Of Wine And Roses*. In fact Withers' song might have served this gritty film better than the Henry Mancini theme song that was actually used, but 'Ain't No Sunshine' came nine years too late for that. It was originally released as a B-side to 'Harlem', a song which it quickly eclipsed to become an award-winner and an all-time favourite.

Same chord, different shape

Now that we're building a repertoire of chord shapes, we're finding more than one way to play various chords.

On page 44 we saw two different ways to play an A minor chord:

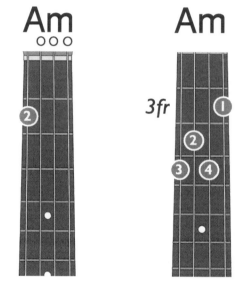

In this next song, we'll use both Am shapes to provide some variety. It also helps us to locate a suitable shape in the context of the other chords.

Take a look at the G chord shape, and you'll see it's pretty easy to move to the Am shape on the 3rd fret from there. But it's even easier to use the other, simpler Am shape to start the song with.

Strumming

The strumming has been kept as simple as possible so you can focus on playing the chords crisply and cleanly. Strum steady down-strums and let the chords ring.

Hidden barre

There are another couple of 'tricks' to make finding chords easier in this song.

Compare the Em and G shapes, and you'll see that they look quite different. There's a 2nd fret barre for the G chord, and moving to it from Em is a bit fiddly.

However, you can form the 2nd fret barre as part of the Em chord too, at which point changing shapes is just a case of lifting off the fourth finger:

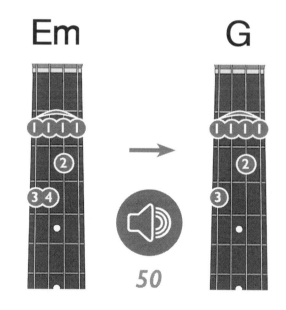

> Chord diagrams usually only *show* one finger dot per string—but that doesn't mean to say you can't also barre across all the strings in preparation for the next chord shape.

Another tip: when moving from Em to Dm, simply play the Dm shape with fingers 2, 3 and 4. They're already in position from the Em shape.

Full chords and lyrics for this song can be found at the back of the book

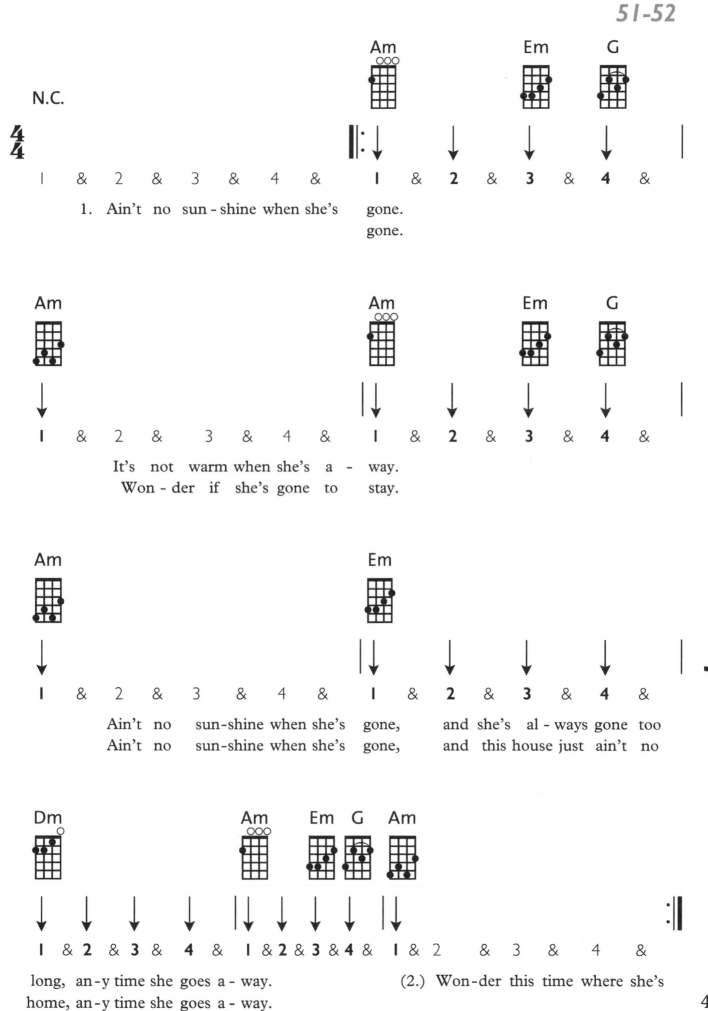

More With Chord Shapes

47

Next-Level Strumming
Working with rhythm notation

Now it's time to explore some more intricate rhythms to bring your strumming to life. Let's start by looking at a few technical terms.

Quarter-notes and eighth-notes

It's very common to play music with four beats in the bar—so far in this book every song apart from 'Mull Of Kintyre' is written this way.

The duration of a note is known as its *value*. The value of a single beat, with four beats in the bar, is a *quarter-note*. Whenever a quarter-note is used to represent a single beat, you'll see '4' at the bottom of the key signature.

Here's a strumming pattern with four quarter-notes: four strums, each worth one beat (see page 31).

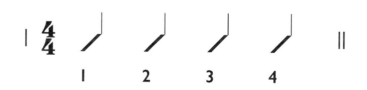

The note values are shown with a *rhythm slash* (the diagonal line) and a *stem* (the attached vertical line).

Notice, by the way, that the strumming direction is not shown. There's no real need, since strumming on a steady beat like this calls for constant down-strums. Optional arrows can be added when things get a bit more complex.

Dividing these quarter-notes in half, as for a typical down-up, down-up strumming pattern, makes a bar of *eighth-notes* (see page 31):

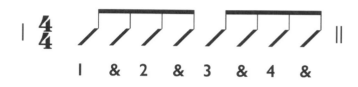

Eighth-notes are connected by a horizontal bar called a *beam*. Showing them in groups of four together makes them easier to read. You'll often see them grouped in pairs, too.

When a single eighth-note is shown on its own, it no longer has a beam, but a *flag* instead.

Quarter- and eighth-note rests

Special symbols known as *rests* are used to show silence of a specific duration.

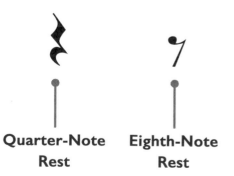

Quarter-Note Rest   Eighth-Note Rest

Reading rhythms

Let's see how this notation works in practice—here's the rhythm from the 'Brown Eyed Girl' strumming pattern again:

Now here's the same thing, written in standard rhythm notation:

In this example, there's a curved line joining two notes together. This *tie* means that the first note of the pair is played, and continues into the second one.

A tie is used when it's easier to show a single note as two values added together. In this case, having a beam split between beats 2 and 3 helps legibility.

The same thing *could* be written this way, but may make it harder to keep track of the beat:

Any value can be modified with a *dot*. A single note worth one-and-a-half beats—which could be written as a quarter-note tied to an eighth-note—can be written as a quarter-note together with a dot instead. The dot means 'half as much again':

Other values

Halving eighth-notes makes ***sixteenth-notes***. Since there are four of these to the beat, they are often used to show fast rhythms and might require careful counting.

Traditionally, they are counted as shown, with the addition of 'e' and 'a' between the standard *"one-and-two-and"* count:

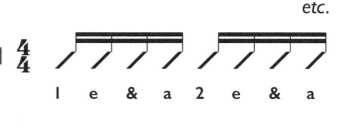

Single sixteenths have two flags; sixteenth rests are likewise modified.

Finally, let's look at longer note values and their rests. The ***half-note*** is worth two quarter-notes:

Half-note rests are written above a line, like so (*right*):

A note worth four beats is a ***whole-note***. It has no stem:

A whole-note rest, hanging from a line, actually indicates any whole bar's rest:

Hey, Soul Sister
Train

Taken from Train's 2009 album *Save Me, San Francisco*, 'Hey, Soul Sister' owes its phenomenal success to a ukulele. Espen Lind suggested that the addition of a uke would make Pat Monahan's bid to write an INXS-flavoured song work better, and quite unexpectedly it did, giving Train their biggest-selling single ever and reaching No. 1 in 16 countries.

Strumming in sixteenth-notes

In theory, strumming in sixteenths is no different from strumming in eighths—the constant down-up, down-up motion is just twice as fast!

However, things do change as the tempo increases. There's less time to think, so it becomes much more important to embed the rhythm pattern as an almost intuitive single gesture—like a flowing phrase made of individual words—rather than focusing on each separate strum in turn.

This is the pattern we'll be playing for 'Hey, Soul Sister'. It's a combination of eighth-notes and sixteenth-notes.

53

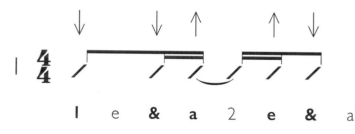

Actually, although it might look more involved than other things we've played so far, it's exactly the same as the 'Brown Eyed Girl' rhythm, but with halved note values—so it's played twice in a single bar.

Remember *"down, down-up, up-down"* from page 34? Try using a more meaningful sentence to vocalise the rhythm and get a good feel for the pattern. How about *"Me, my-self, and I"*? Or maybe *"Tea, cof-fee, and milk"*. You'll doubtless come up with better examples yourself!

Simplifying the music

In fact, as long as the strumming pattern is repeated, it's not necessary to write the whole thing out for every bar.

We can get a lot more music on the page if, once the pattern's established, we just write simple rhythm slashes to indicate the beat:

Chord shapes

'Hey, Soul Sister' uses just four different chords, in a couple of repeating sequence. Here's the sequence for the verse, with each chord played for one bar:

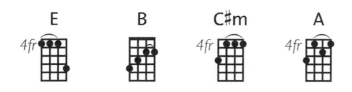

Apart from B, all the chords are barred at the 4th fret. Here's another useful way to play E.

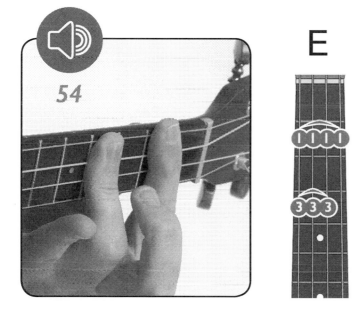

This shape uses two barres. The first finger lays across the 2nd fret across all four strings, and the third finger is on the 4th fret on the 2nd, 3rd and 4th strings.

It might take a bit of getting used to, but once you get the knack you'll be using this shape all the time up and down the neck.

Your third finger will need to bend slightly inside-out for this barre. You don't have to be double-jointed to do this, but you will need to be relaxed and confident.

Above all, check that you have an optimum left-hand position, with the wrist kept low and the thumb staying towards the back of the neck.

Of course, in standard chord diagrams, you won't see two barres played on top of each other like this. But—as we saw on page 46—that doesn't mean to say you can't play a shape that way.

So when you see this in the music (*right*), feel free to add a barre at the back of the shape to support the main fretting finger.

As with any barre chord, it can be played anywhere else on the neck too. Up one fret, it makes an F chord...

... and moving it *down* two frets—losing the first finger barre—it's actually the same D we saw on page 22, but now barred (*right*).

Barring with the first finger simply helps support the third finger barre. It's easier than fretting just the top string with the first finger. Also, changing to the B chord becomes much more straightforward.

Hey, Soul Sister

Train

Next-Level Strumming

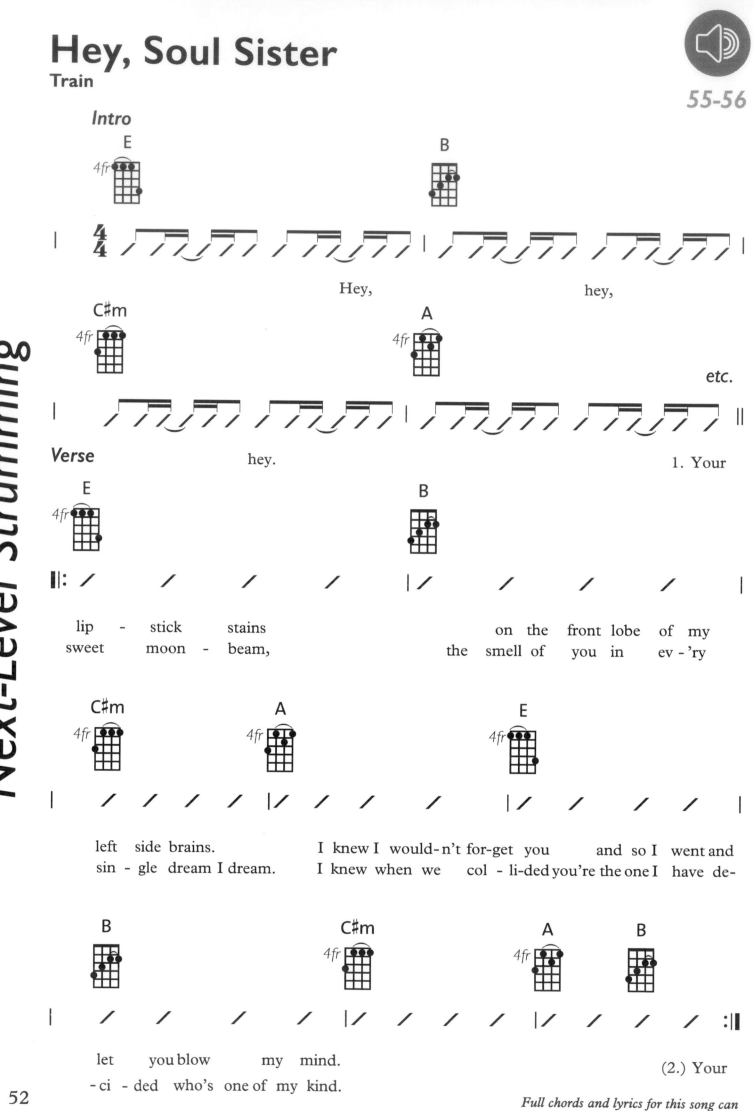

Intro

Hey, hey, hey.

Verse

1. Your

lip - stick stains on the front lobe of my
sweet moon - beam, the smell of you in ev - 'ry

left side brains. I knew I would-n't for-get you and so I went and
sin - gle dream I dream. I knew when we col - li-ded you're the one I have de-

let you blow my mind.
-ci - ded who's one of my kind.

(2.) Your

*Full chords and lyrics for this song can
be found at the back of the book*

Chorus

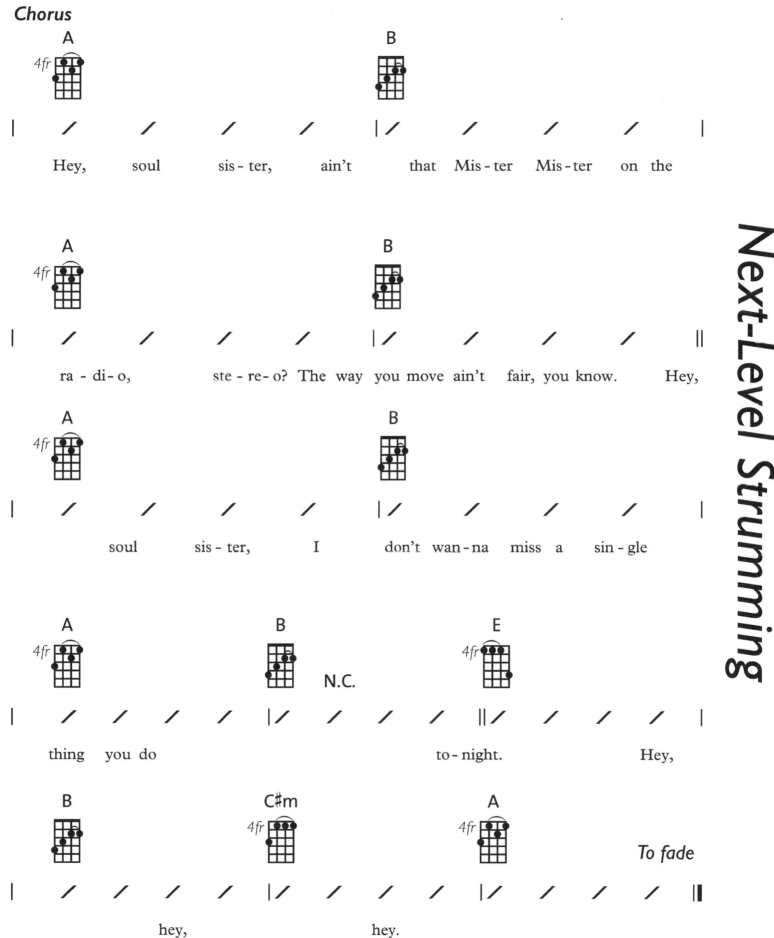

Hey, soul sis-ter, ain't that Mis-ter Mis-ter on the

ra-di-o, ste-re-o? The way you move ain't fair, you know. Hey,

soul sis-ter, I don't wan-na miss a sin-gle

thing you do to-night. Hey,

hey, hey.

Walk On The Wild Side

Lou Reed

Lou Reed's album *Transformer* caused quite a stir when it was released in 1972 and 'Walk on the Wild Side' was its defining track. In it Reed sketched his acquaintances' various migrations to New York from the provinces, touching on topics not normally sung about on radio music stations. Nothing, though, could stop Reed's bass-driven, girl group-backed song with its haunting fade-out sax solo from becoming a hit.

Strumming constant sixteenth-notes

This song will put your strumming to the test!

16 individual strums in a single bar can sound a bit monotonous, so try to create a bit of interest by *accenting* (stressing) the first strum of each beat.

You can achieve this by playing more loudly on the beat but, most importantly, playing fainter strums on the other three sixteenths—something like this:

Those little ＞ symbols above the first sixteenth of each beat are *accents*.

The only new shape for this song is the F (*below*). It's just like the original shape from page 19 but with an additional note on the top string—you can keep it there as long as you're moving between C and F.

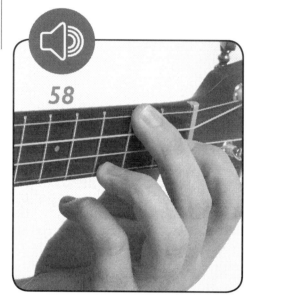

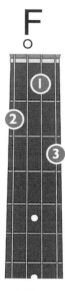
F

57
etc.

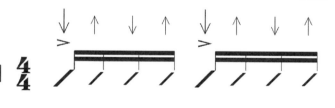

Intro

C   F

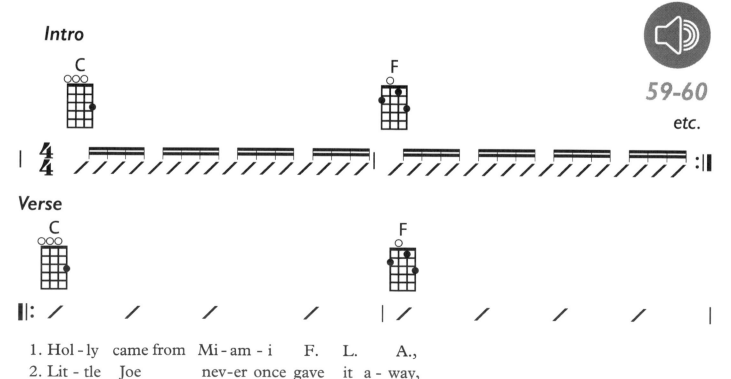

59-60

etc.

Verse

C   F

1. Hol - ly   came from   Mi - am - i   F.   L.   A.,
2. Lit - tle   Joe   nev-er once gave   it a - way,

Full chords and lyrics for this song can be found at the back of the book

C   F

| / / / / | / / / / |

hitch-hiked her way a-cross the U. S. A.,
ev - 'ry - bo - dy had to pay and pay,

C   Dm   F   Dm

| / / / / | / / / / ‖

plucked her eye-brows on the way, shaved her legs and then he was a she, she says,
hus-tle here and a hus-tle there, New York Ci-ty's the place where they say,

Chorus

C   F

| / / / / | / / / / |

"Hey, babe, take a walk on the wild side." I said,
"Hey, babe, take a walk on the wild side." I said,

C   F

| / / / / | / / / / |

"Hey, hon-ey, take a walk on the wild side."
"Hey, ba - by, take a walk on the wild side."

C   F   C   F   *To fade*

| / / / / | / / / / | / / / / | / / / / :‖

Seventh Chords
Looking at chord relationships

In this section we'll take a closer look at **seventh** chords—what makes them tick and how to play them. They play an important part in the repertoire of chord shapes on the uke.

The story so far
Up till now, we've seen two different *seventh* (7) shapes. G^7 (page 19) and D^7 (page 32).

We also saw how both of these shapes could be barred and played higher up the neck (*right*):

The seventh sound
For a quick demonstration of the way this type of chord works, play through 'Jambalaya' (opposite). This song uses just two chords, C and G^7, in a simple repeating chord sequence.

Listen to the way the chords relate to each other. G^7 seems to 'lead' to C—if you play G^7 on its own it feels like it's hanging in the air until you play a C chord. It's as though, having played G^7, you *expect* to hear C.

This has to do with the individual notes in G^7. Without getting into too much detail, certain notes in the G^7 chord react together to create a kind of tension.

This tension is then released by playing the C chord. In music we say that the tension is **resolved**.

Understanding a little about the relationship between these two chords allows you build your own chord sequences, and helps to work out the chords to songs—you'll start to 'hear' these connections between chords.

It's also really useful when you want to put songs in a different **key**.

Starting to transpose
Now try this: play 'Jambalaya' again, but this time instead of G^7 play D^7 using the shape shown (*left*). And instead of C, play a G chord (using whichever shape suits you best).

You'll hear that the two new chords, D^7 and G, relate to each other in the same way that G^7 and C do. If you play D^7, you expect to hear G after it—D^7 leads to G.

This means that you've successfully **transposed** the song: you've used a different set of chords but maintained the relationships between them—so it still *sounds* like 'Jambalaya', but with the melody at a different pitch.

This is a great skill to have if you find that a particular song isn't in the right range for you.

Overleaf we'll look at more seventh chords and how they relate to chords around them.

Full chords and lyrics for this song can be found at the back of the book

Jambalaya (On The Bayou)

Hank Williams

'Jambalaya' is an uncharacteristically upbeat Hank Williams number that has fun with Cajun names. It is rumoured that Williams co-wrote the song with Texas-born country pianist Moon Mullican who remained uncredited but may have been compensated with royalties. Either way, the combination of its bouncy melody and Louisiana patois resulted in countless other versions by artists ranging from Jo Stafford to The Carpenters.

61-62

Seventh Chords

N.C. | C | | etc.

Good-bye Joe, me got-ta go, me oh
- lay', craw-fish pie, and fi - le

G⁷

my - oh. Me got-ta go, pole the
gum - bo. For to - night I'm gon - na

C

pir - ogue down the bay - ou. My Y -
see my cher a - mie - oh. Pick guit -

G⁷

- vonne, sweet-est one, me oh my - oh.
- ar, fill fruit jar, and be gay - oh.

Son of a gun we'll have big
Son of a gun we'll have big

C

fun on the bay - ou. *(Chorus)* Jam - ba -
fun on the bay - ou.

More seventh shapes

There are five common *seventh* (7) shapes on the uke, and we've already looked at two of them. Here are the other three.

First of all, a shape for C7 that can easily be barred up the neck:

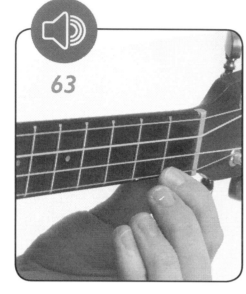 

C7

And another, A7, that's also really easy to play as a barred shape:

A7

Take a look at the shapes at the top of the next page to see how all these seventh shapes are barred.

Lastly, here's a shape for E7 that uses three fingers:

E7

Barring this one is a bit more involved. As you've already got three fretted strings in this shape, you just need to fret the remaining open string to play it up the neck. Here it is one fret higher, making F7:

F7

This shape makes a lovely, full sound and really comes into its own further up the neck. Try it two frets higher as a G7, for instance.

Recap

Here are the five different *seventh* shapes we've seen, together with the barred versions of each—in this example the barred versions are played two frets higher than the original.

Original

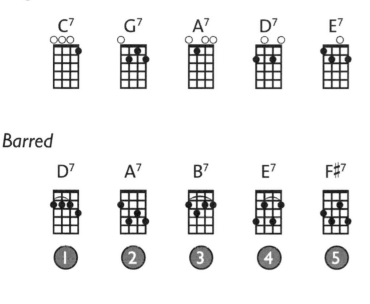

Barred

Here's the next pair. Try playing the A⁷ with the first finger already barring at the 2nd fret. As with the previous pair, you can keep the barring finger in position for both chords:

Next, a seventh shape that moves to the major shape we saw on page 51. Again, you can keep the barre in position to move from one chord to the other:

Pairing chord shapes

These different *seventh* shapes naturally move to specific *major* chord shapes.

Move backwards and forwards between these two shapes a few times to hear and feel how they 'belong' together.

For the first one, you'll notice that you can keep the barring finger in position:

And the next pair—you might have guessed that you can keep the barring finger in position for both chords here, too:

Here's the last one. Get the barring finger ready on the 2nd fret and keep it in position:

> Try moving all these pairs of shapes up the neck to hear how they still fit together. You could use each pair to play 'Jambalaya'— you'll soon hear if you're playing them right.

Seventh Chords

Dominant-tonic relationship

The pairs of chords we've just been looking at are connected by something called the **dominant-tonic relationship**. It sounds grand but it's really quite simple.

The chords in each pair are separated by a certain distance known as a **fifth**. That's the distance between any note and a note that's alphabetically five away (*see opposite*).

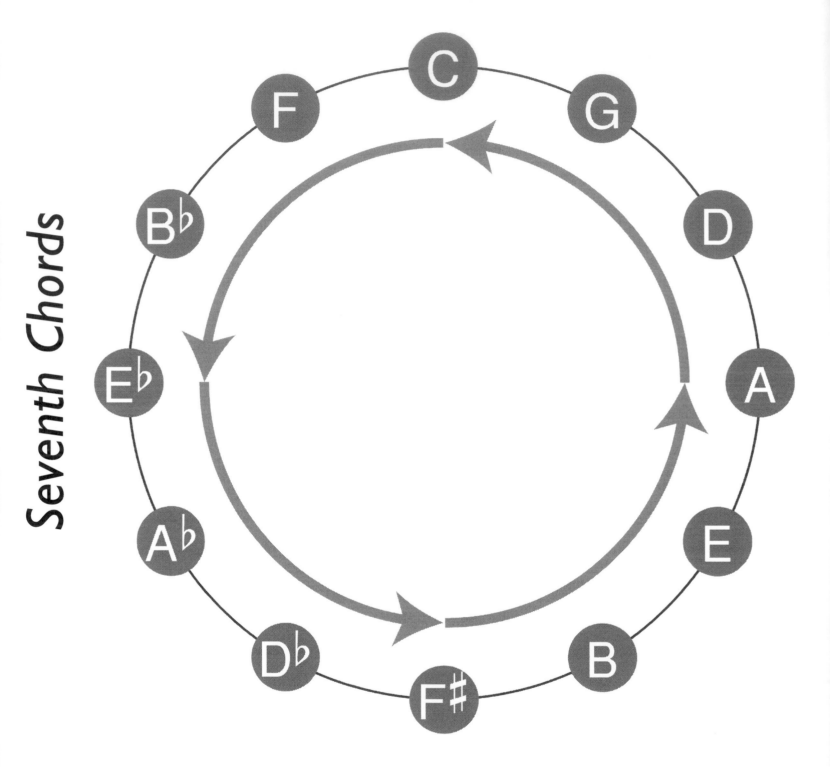

The circle of fifths

These *dominant-tonic* pairs of chords are displayed in a handy diagram, (*above*), called the **circle of fifths**.

Moving anti-clockwise one step, you'll move from **chord five** (V) to **chord one** (I). Try finding E^7 to A, for example, or C^7 to F.

Seventh Chords

Moving in fifths

Counting from A, for example, the note a *fifth* away is E:

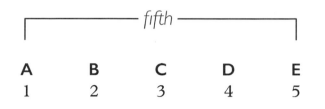

			fifth			
A	B	C	D	E
1	2	3	4	5

Or, if you were counting up from C, the note a fifth away is a G:

			fifth			
C	D	E	F	G
1	2	3	4	5

Counting this way means that we can also number the chords. In the above example G is **chord five** (V), also called the '**dominant**' chord, while C is **chord one** (I), also called the '**tonic**' chord.

Every *chord I* has a companion *chord V*. We've seen a few of them: G^7 to C; B^7 to E; A^7 to D; $F^{\#7}$ to B and so on.

> So really all we're talking about here is **chord V** 'going' to **chord I**.
>
> Make sure that chord V is a **7** type—so G is G^7, for instance—to create the tension that is then *resolved* with chord one.
>
> The concept of chord V7 going to chord I is at the heart of the way chords join together in **chord progressions**.

Crazy
Patsy Cline

When Patsy Cline was casting around for a song to follow her 1961 hit 'I Fall To Pieces' she was offered 'Crazy' written by Willie Nelson. She disliked it, partly because Nelson's own version featured his perfunctory vocal with the words almost spoken ahead of the melody line. She was persuaded to reconsider and duly had a hit with what turned out to be a subtle and sophisticated song that would become a standard.

Chord choices

This arrangement of the country ballad, 'Crazy', contains most of the *dominant* shapes we've just studied.

Often (not always, it's true) these *dominant* chords go on to their appropriate *tonic* chords.

Go through the chord sequence to 'Crazy' and see how many dominant-tonic moves you can spot.

Notice that A^7 goes to Dm, rather than D. It still 'works', since in fact a dominant chord can go to a major *or* minor tonic chord.

> ### Recap
>
> We know about three different chord types: *major*, *minor* and *seventh*. Seventh chords contain tension that is released by going either to a major or minor chord.
>
> When this tension-and-release takes place between two chords, they are said to be in a *dominant-tonic relationship*.

Take another look at the *dominant-tonic* pairs on page 59. If you're up for a challenge, try using different shapes for the dominant chords—and then using the appropriate nearest shape for the tonic chords.

Of course, you can also mix-and-match—any G^7 shape will still 'go' to any other C shape, for example—but it might not always sound quite so smooth.

Crazy
Patsy Cline

Diminished Chords

There's a new chord type in this song: the **diminished** chord. This shape crops up in all sorts of country, blues and jazz songs.

The theory behind diminished ('*dim*') chords is too involved to go into here, but there's one thing you should know: a diminished chord can have lots of different names. You'll see a chord shape called Cdim, for example, and then a few bars later you might well see the same shape called Adim or F#dim! Take a look at page 98 for more info.

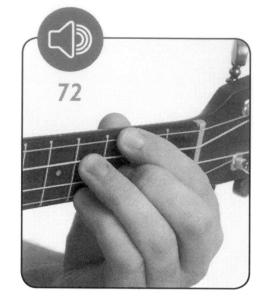

72

C#dim

Seventh Chords

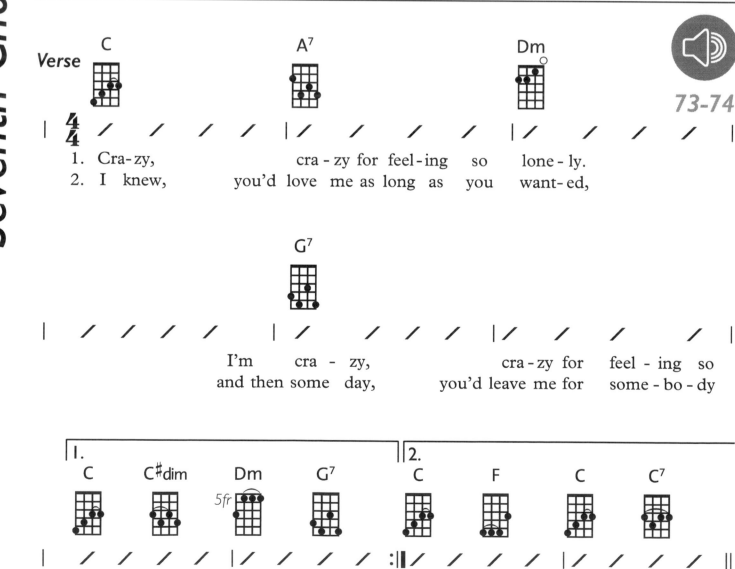

73-74

Verse

C   A⁷   Dm

1. Cra-zy,   cra - zy for feel-ing   so   lone - ly.
2. I knew,   you'd love me as long as   you   want- ed,

G⁷

I'm   cra - zy,   cra-zy for   feel - ing so
and then some   day,   you'd leave me for   some - bo - dy

1.
C   C#dim   Dm   G⁷

blue.

2.
C   F   C   C⁷

new.

Full chords and lyrics for this song can be found at the back of the book

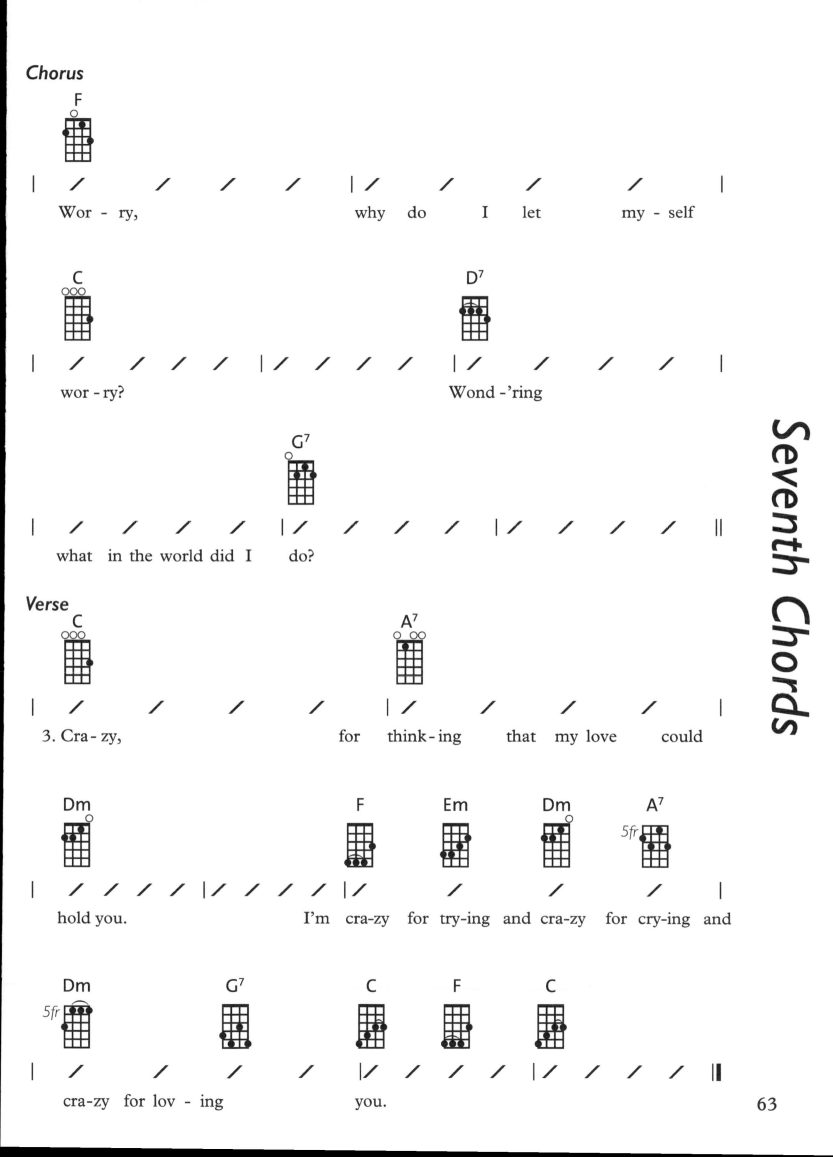

Playing Triplets
Splitting the beat into three

Up till now we've looked at rhythms that split the beat into two—or four—so we've worked with quarter-notes, eighth-notes and sixteenth-notes.

But it's also possible to split the beat into three, creating **triplets**. In this section we're going to look at how to write triplets, how to count them, read them and of course play them too.

New time signatures

The time signature of the music so far has overwhelmingly been 4/4, with one song in 3/4.

The top number of a time signature tells us how many beats there are in the bar; the bottom number determines what kind of note is used to represent one beat.

In 3/4, for instance, there are three beats to the bar, with each beat worth a quarter-note.

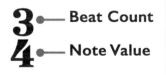

The lower number also tells us *how* the beat divides. Take a look at this example, with a **6/8** time signature. We know from the numbers that we have six eighth-notes to each bar.

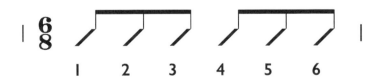

In 6/8, though, there's an important feature: the notes are grouped into threes. In fact, 6/8 is more commonly counted as *two* beats, each split into three: *"one-and-a, two-and-a"*.

Time Signature Types

Time signatures that subdivide the beat into two are called **simple** time signatures. They have **4** as the lower number.

Time signatures that subdivide into three are called **compound** time signatures. They have **8** as the lower number.

So, if 6/8 really has only two beats, and each beat is made of three eighth-notes, how do we write a single beat? Take a look:

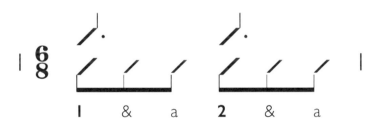

A single beat in 6/8 is written as a dotted quarter-note. If you're used to reading music in 4/4, you'll think of a dotted quarter-note as one-and-a-half beats, so it might take a moment to get to grips with 6/8!

There are other compound time signatures too—**9/8** and **12/8** crop up occasionally. In every case, the basic beat is shown as a dotted quarter-note, with subdivisions shown as eighth-notes.

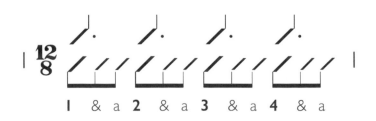

Strumming in compound time

In simple time such as 3/4 and 4/4, the strumming direction is pretty much always obvious: **down** on the beat and **up** in between ('off' the beat). That way, the hand is always alternating and each strum sets the hand up for the next strum.

But in 6/8 it's not so easy. Here's what happens if we alternate the strum direction:

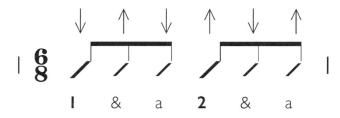

Try playing a few bars through, and you'll see that the second beat is played with an up-strum.

This isn't a real problem, but it might feel a bit counter-intuitive, and you might find it takes a bit of concentration to place an accent on the second beat.

If you're not careful, strumming alternately this way can sound more like 3/4 than 6/8. Try the exercise at the bottom of the page to sharpen up your sense of compound time.

If you want to ensure that you're strumming down *on* the beat, you'll need start *every* beat with a down-strum:

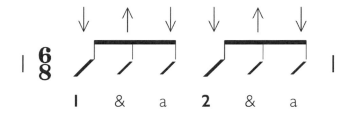

This raises another issue, of course—you end up playing the final strum of the previous beat and the first strum of the new beat as consecutive down-strums.

It's easy to get your hand in a muddle, and that really doesn't help the music to flow, either.

Accenting the beats

Try this simple exercise to develop a feel for compound time. Strum in even eighth-notes, grouping them in threes—as for a 6/8 time signature.

Now, while still strumming, shift the accents so that you're playing pairs of notes instead.

Six eighth-notes in the bar can either mean 6/8 or 3/4, and you should be able switch from one to the other easily.

Ensure the accent is at the start of each beat so you're clearly defining groups of three for 6/8 and groups of two for 3/4.

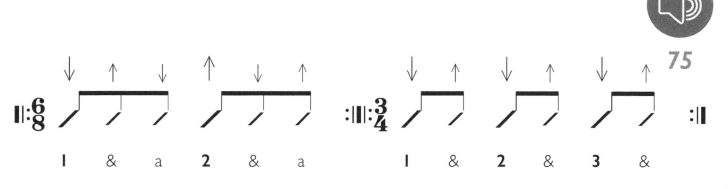

75

65

Playing Triplets

The split stroke

Strumming triplets is made a lot easier by introducing the thumb to strum with. In the split stroke, three separate movements combine to play a triplet.

76

Start by playing a standard down-strum with the index finger:

Follow up with another down-strum, this time with the thumb:

Finish off with an up-strum with the finger again.

An alternative method

There are a few variations on the split stroke. You could also try playing triplets using just the finger, which is how George Formby devotees generally play it.

Play a standard down-strum, as in the previous example:

Now strum up, again with the finger, but stroking just the top string:

Finally, strum down onto just the bottom string:

Whichever method you settle on, you'll build up a strumming technique that will begin to feel like a single gesture rather than a series of separate movements.

In the *first version*, adding the thumb means you're actually just moving the strumming hand down-up, down-up as usual (but now providing *two* strums in the 'down' part).

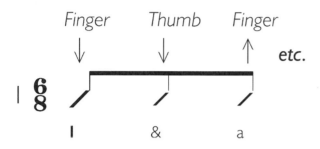

Practise moving the strumming finger down while holding the thumb back until it's needed. It won't seem natural to begin with, but after a while you'll naturally hold the thumb in position, ready to follow the finger.

You might also try playing the final strum—the up-strum—with the back of the thumb instead, as a guitarist might.

In the *second version*, the effect relies on selectively strumming just the outer strings at certain points: the 1st string on the second strum, and the 4th string on the third strum.

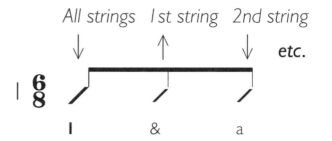

This requires a fair bit of control, and inevitably creates more emphasis on the first strum, since it's the only one that plays all four strings. This defines the beat very clearly.

So, experiment until you find a technique that suits you best. As long as you're playing (and thinking) in triplets, you needn't worry whether you're doing it 'right'.

Of course, if you're playing an even number of strums within a beat, there's no need to attempt split strokes. There are plenty of strumming patterns in compound time that can be played with straightforward alternating down-strums and up-strums.

Here's a common 6/8 pattern, which starts with an eighth-note followed by four sixteenths. This then repeats. This is strummed 'down, down-up-down-up'.

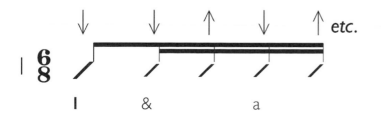

You'll see this pattern in the intro and verse of 'Norwegian Wood' (*overleaf*), and combined with the split stroke in the chorus.

> Uke legend **Jake Shimabukuro**, by the way, plays triplet split strokes by strumming **down** with the finger, then **up** with the thumb, followed by the finger.
>
> It's your call—just find a technique that works for you!

77

Norwegian Wood (This Bird Has Flown)
The Beatles

With its oblique lyric, 'Norwegian Wood' started life as John Lennon's attempt to write a non-explicit song about an extra-marital affair. Paul McCartney added the reference to the pine interior that was trendy at the time and George Harrison made his recording debut on the sitar. The enigmatic words, with their hint of a revenge arson attack plus the then-unfamiliar sound of Harrison's sitar, made this a stand-out track on the famous *Rubber Soul* album.

The split stroke

This Beatles song in 6/8 is perfect for getting used to the time signature and for trying your hand at split strokes.

The suggested strumming pattern, shown in the intro, works perfectly for the verse, and we'll see it in the chorus too. It's the pattern shown on the previous page.

But the chorus also has a change of feel, and we can reflect that with a different pattern.

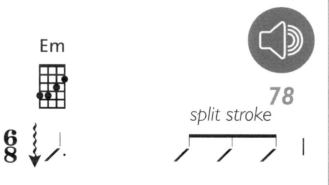

78

split stroke

Start the bar with a single, exaggerated down-strum. The wavy arrow indicates that the strings should be heard individually, so strum across the strings very deliberately.

The second half of the bar has a split stroke. You're free to play this with whichever technique you've settled on.

It's fairly slow, so it's not difficult, and you'll have the long strum at the beginning of the bar to give you a bit of time to prepare.

After two bars the strumming returns to the original pattern; then these four bars repeat. You could also play the split stroke throughout the chorus if you prefer.

> ### D.S. al Fine
>
> A variation on *D.C. al Fine* that we saw on page 42, **D.S.** means 'from the sign' (dal segno).
>
> The 'sign' is the 𝄋 at the beginning of the verse. Play to the end of the chorus and return to the sign to play the second verse.

79-80

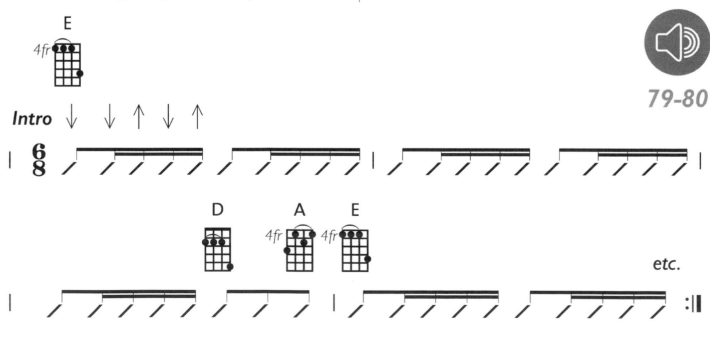

Playing Triplets

68

Full chords and lyrics for this song can be found at the back of the book

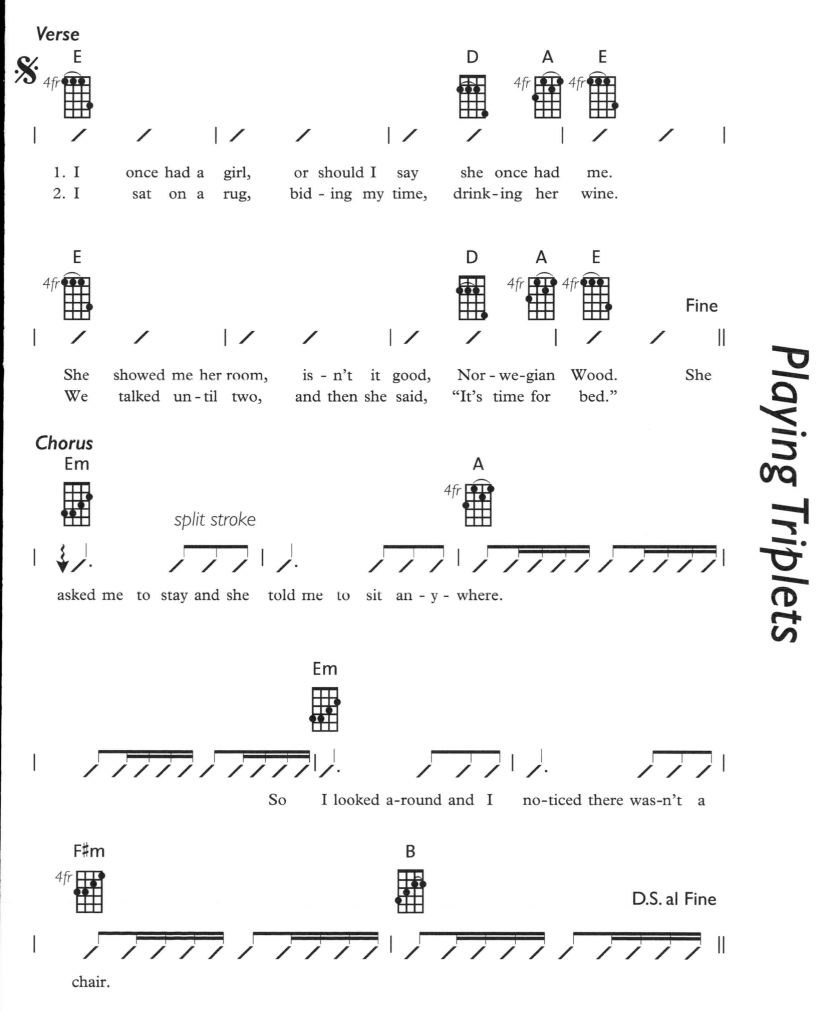

Blueberry Hill

Fats Domino

'Blueberry Hill', originally written in 1940 for a movie starring singing cowboy Gene Autry, was soon covered by several other artists. It was not until 1956, however, that it was recorded by Antoine 'Fats' Domino. 'Blueberry Hill' was many people's introduction to Domino's irresistible New Orleans accent and his equally irresistible rolling piano style. The song became a rock 'n' roll classic.

12/8 feel

This '50s ballad is a great example of the typical 12/8 feel. This time signature is characterised by four strong, even beats, with clearly-defined triplets within each beat.

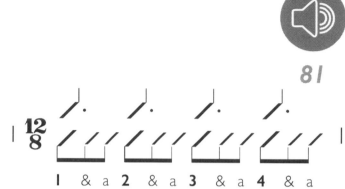

81

To achieve the solid rhythm, play a split stroke on every single beat. It's hard work, and will be a real test of your technique.

Try it on a single chord, building up the tempo slowly—soon it'll 'click', and you'll get the hang of it.

Chord shape choices

Notice that E, Em, B and F#7 can all be played with a barre at the 2nd fret, keeping everything close at hand.

> **D.S. al Coda**
>
> As before, we have the 𝄋 sign at the beginning of the verse. This time, though, rather than continuing until the 'Fine', the song jumps to the **Coda** (literally the 'tail') at the end of the third verse.
>
> The coda, indicated with the ⊕ symbol, is found at the bottom of the page opposite.

Take a break

Where N.C. (*no chord*) written, stop strumming until another chord diagram appears.

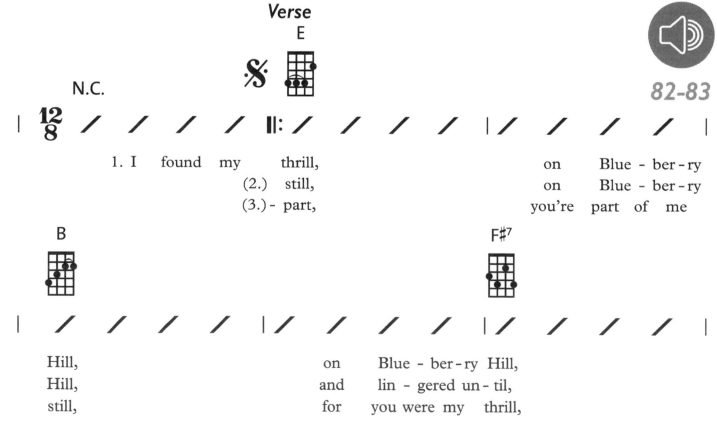

82-83

70

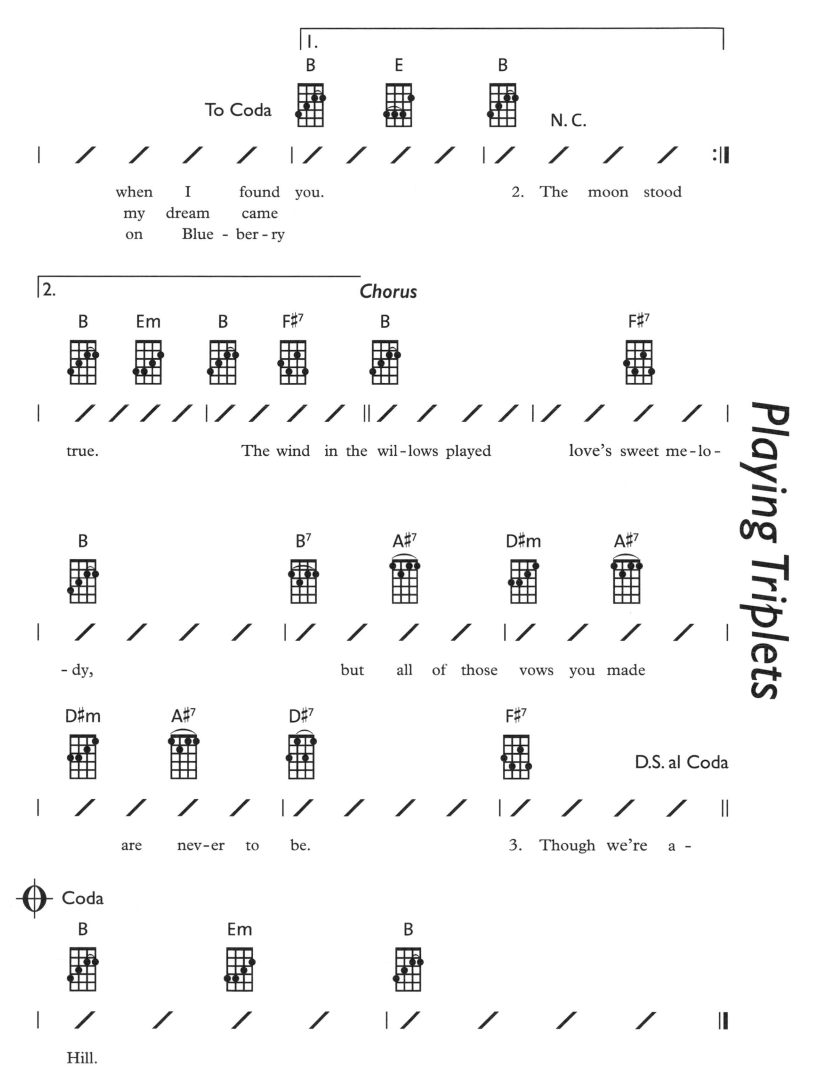

Reading Tablature
Strings and frets

Uke music can be written using a system called *tablature*. Also called 'tab', it's the traditional method for stringed instruments and very easy to learn.

String Lines

In ukulele tablature, each string is represented by a horizontal line, as if the uke were lying on its side, like this:

Tab Notation

Various musical symbols are used, much like in standard notation (*below*):

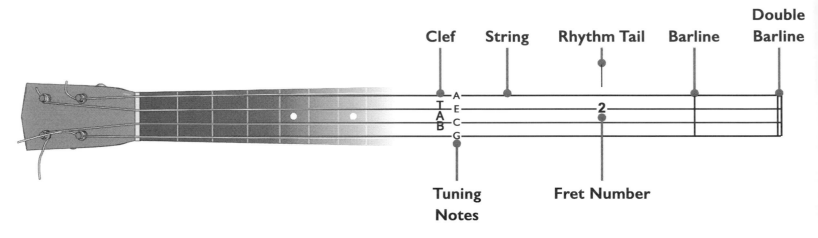

The *clef* simply tells you you're reading tablature, and the *tuning notes* are only generally included if the music is written for a different uke tuning than the standard G-C-E-A.

Lots of tab written for the ukulele doesn't use *rhythm tails* at all, so you won't necessarily know how long a note should last or exactly where in the bar it's played.

We're including rhythm tails because it makes all that much clearer. The tails are exactly the same as the ones we looked at on page 48.

The note head is a number, which represents a fret. The note shown in the example shows the 2nd string played at the 2nd fret.

Of course, it's easy to show more than one note at a time in tab, too. Here's a bar with a C chord played once, followed by half a bar each of F and G⁷.

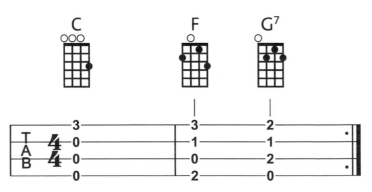

Notice that repeat barlines, time signatures and chord diagrams can all be used in the usual way in tablature.

Scales

Now that we've got a way to write individual notes, we can write scales, tunes, fingerpicking patterns or any other kind of specific combinations of notes we need.

Here's a C major *scale*. Pick each note in turn, starting with the open 3rd string. You should end up on the 3rd fret of the top string:

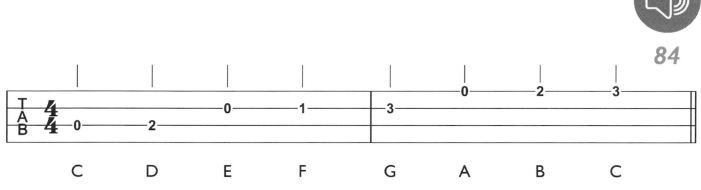

Now for a bit of a challenge: it's the intro for 'Brown Eyed Girl' on page 35. For almost the whole four bars, you'll need to play two notes together.

Pick the lower note with the thumb, and the upper note with the first or second finger, so you're almost *pinching* the notes together.

Remember: only the first note in a pair of tied notes is actually played. The second note just extends the duration of the note (page 49).

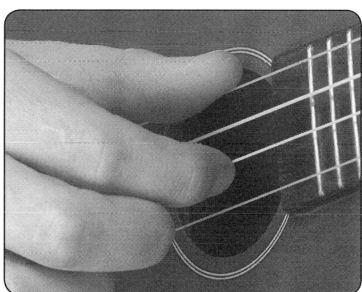

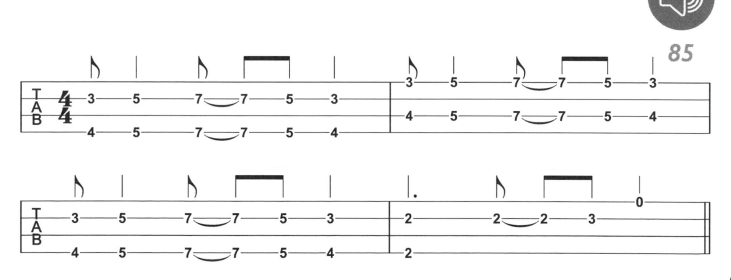

Notes and Scales

Sorting out those sharps and flats

In the section on reading tablature (page 72), we saw a C major scale. Here it is again. Notice that all the notes are arranged in alphabetical order, starting on C and continuing on up until we reach C again.

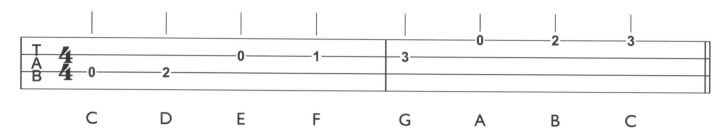

As discussed on page 39, note names are all two frets apart, except for B-C and E-F. Let's look a bit more closely at the way the C major scale is structured.

It might not be obvious when we're using more than one string to play a scale, but in fact all the notes are two frets apart except for B-C and E-F. F is on the 1st fret of the E string, and C is just one fret higher than B.

We can plot out the C major scale in terms of the interval used:

C   Tone   D   Tone   E | Semitone | F   Tone   G   Tone   A   Tone   B | Semitone | C

Play the scale through again, and see if you can here that the distance between E-F, for example, is smaller than the distance between C-D. This classic combination of intervals is the same for every major scale and the sequence *"tone-tone-semitone-tone-tone-tone-semitone"* is worth learning off by heart.

Tones and Semitones

The interval of two frets is a **tone**, while the interval of one fret is a **semitone**, the smallest commonly-used interval in Western music.

Adding sharps

The formula for building a major scale is always the same, no matter where you start. Here's a G major scale (*below*).

There are lots of places to play different notes on the uke, but for this example, we're just moving the C major scale (*opposite*) up the neck until it starts on G.

Key Signature

The number of sharps or flats used in a scale is known as the **key signature**. Every major scale has a unique key signature.

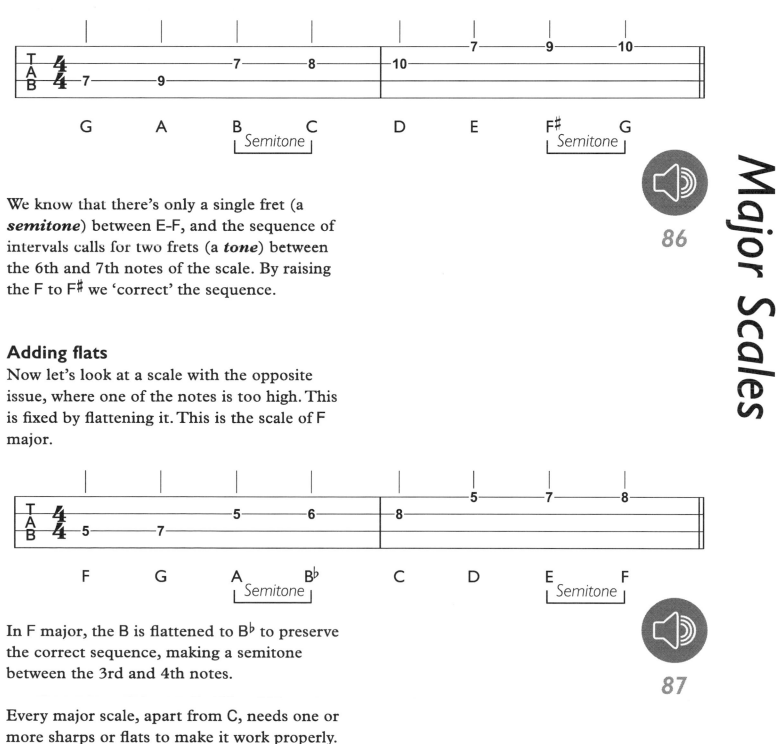

We know that there's only a single fret (a **semitone**) between E-F, and the sequence of intervals calls for two frets (a **tone**) between the 6th and 7th notes of the scale. By raising the F to F# we 'correct' the sequence.

Adding flats

Now let's look at a scale with the opposite issue, where one of the notes is too high. This is fixed by flattening it. This is the scale of F major.

In F major, the B is flattened to B♭ to preserve the correct sequence, making a semitone between the 3rd and 4th notes.

Every major scale, apart from C, needs one or more sharps or flats to make it work properly. Try starting on any note and see how many sharps or flats you use.

Major Scales

Notes on the Neck

Here are the names of all the notes up to the 12th fret—at which point the notes start again as if from the 1st fret.

There are a few things to notice:

- There are sharps and flats between all pairs of ordinary note names except between B-C and E-F, since these pairs are only a semitone (one fret) apart.

- You can easily see the *"tone-tone-semitone-tone-tone-tone-semitone"* sequence making a C major scale starting on the open 3rd string.

- The note names repeat from the 12th fret—an *octave* higher. You can hear that these notes 'sound' somehow the same as the originals despite being higher.

- The 4th string is pitched a *fifth* higher than the 3rd string; while the 2nd string is pitched a *third* higher than the 3rd string. The top string is a *fourth* above the 2nd string. The top string, then, is just a tone higher than the bottom string.

Sharps and Flats

'In between' notes can have flat names and sharp names: A♭ and G♯ are the same note. These alternatives are called **enharmonic equivalents**.

Weirdly, in some circumstances, you'll find C called B♯, and E called F♭, and so on.

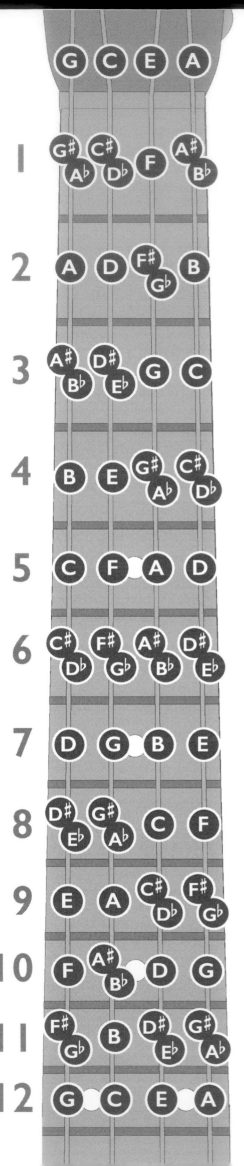

Notes and Scales

Fingering scales and tunes

Take another look at the scales on page 75 and you'll see that every note is fretted within a range of four frets.

There's a good reason for this: with four left-hand fingers available, each finger can be assigned to a different fret, and the whole scale can be played without moving each finger from its designated position.

Here's the F scale again, with fingering numbers also written in, above each note.

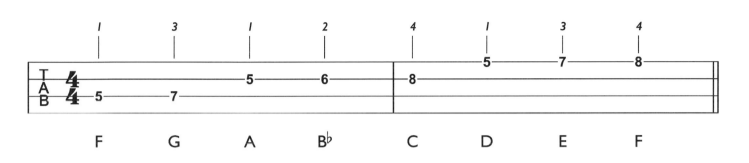

Since most tunes use notes of one scale, it's worth getting to grips with the idea of specific fingerings. Here's the original intro figure for 'Redemption Song' (page 24), which can all be played in a single hand position:

88

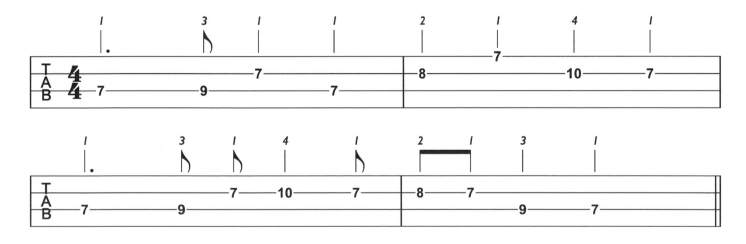

All these notes can be played elsewhere on the neck, too—but this way your hand can stay in a single, compact shape.

By the way, you might find it easiest if you barre across the top three strings with your first finger throughout this little exercise.

Fingerpicking
Playing patterns

To create a more subtle accompaniment than is generally possible with strumming, the fingers of the right hand can pick individual strings in combination. This is known as *fingerpicking*.

Fingerpicking basics

The right-hand fingers and thumb should be free to move over the strings, with the back of the hand held in a relaxed, gentle curve. The overall position won't be very different from an ideal strumming position, but ensure that the fingers are hanging loosely over the strings.

Place the thumb on the 4th string, with the tip (or the nail) just poised on the string. The thumb is used to pick both the 4th and 3rd string, so make sure it can move freely from one string to the other.

The first finger picks the 2nd string, with the second finger picking the top string.

Let's try a very simple fingerpicking pattern on a basic C chord shape. This pattern of picked notes starts on the lowest-sounding string—the 3rd string—and goes up in pitch to the top string.

Nails or Not?

If you have a strong set of fingernails, you can make good use of them in fingerpicking, but they're not essential. The soft strings of the uke can easily be picked by the fleshy underside of the fingertips, too.

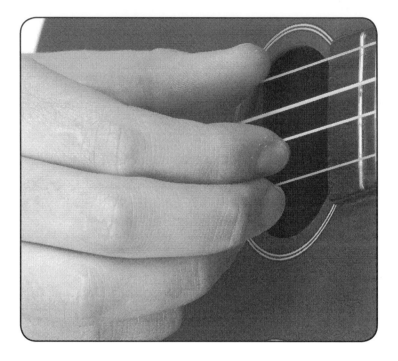

The finger numbers (with 'T' for the thumb) are shown below the notes.

89

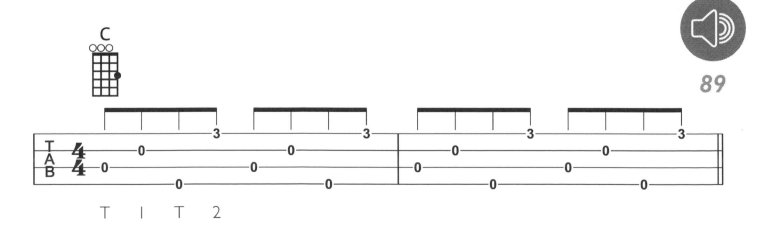

78

Fingerpicking Exercise

Play through this chord sequence on the same picking pattern. Take it at whatever speed you like, building it up when it feels comfortable, letting the picked notes flow into each other.

There's a new chord towards the end: G⁷sus⁴. Place your fingers for the following G⁷ in advance, but add your fourth finger on the 3rd fret of the top string.

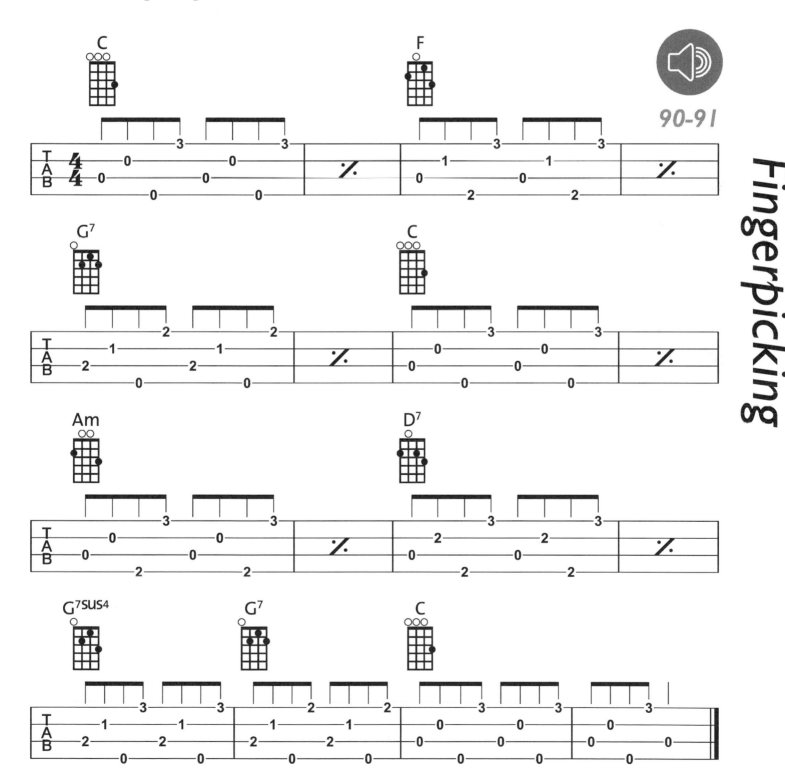

90-91

Further patterns

Assuming it's used to accompany singing, or to provide an additional texture with other instruments, a fingerpicking pattern needs to be:

- **Unobtrusive**. It's not a solo feature, but something that happens in the background.

- **Steady**. The fingerpicking provides a rhythmic element, so it needs to be reliable—which probably means it should also be simple.

- **Versatile**. Ideally, you'll want to keep your picking pattern going smoothly, whichever chord comes along.

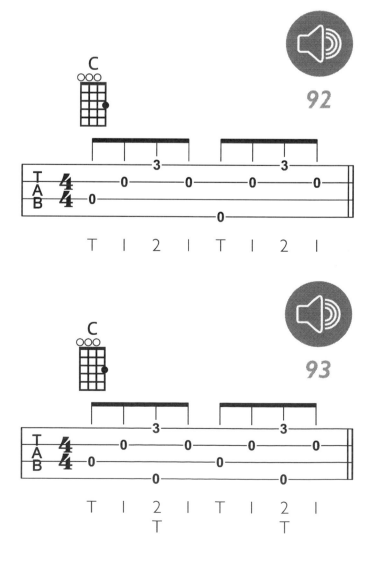

> **Repertoire of Patterns**
>
> This all means that most picking patterns will be fairly straightforward, unless you're planning on making a feature of the uke, perhaps in an instrumental section or solo part. In fact, you might find you never use more than two or three different fingerpicking patterns.

Here is another suggestion, again played in eighths (*right*).

Try playing this pattern with the chord sequence on page 79, and experiment with accenting the notes in different ways. It can give you an interesting new perspective on a familiar picking pattern.

Here's another (*right*). This one has two notes played together on the second beat, which means 'pinching' the two outer strings together with thumb and finger as for the 'Brown Eyed Girl' intro on page 73. You'll see this pattern in 'Yesterday' (page 82).

The idea is to let the individual notes of the pattern flow together until you hear a continuous ripple rather than a sequence of separate notes.

Finger combinations

So far, we've been using the first and second fingers on the top two strings, with the thumb on the bottom two strings.

This works well because the lower notes (on the 3rd and 4th strings) are generally on strong beats—the 1st and 3rd beats—and using the thumb to pick notes on these beats can help to create a very solid and regular sound.

However, in some picking patterns, you might find it works better to keep the thumb on the 4th string but use three different fingers—one for each of the upper strings (*right*).

Let's play through acouple of examples of patterns that might be more suitable for this kind of fingering.

Fingerpicking

The exercise on page 79 uses an **arpeggio** of the C chord shape—all of the notes of the chord in order of pitch. This pattern (*right*), in 3/4, includes the arpeggio idea up and down again. Although the notes flow perfectly, the order of the picking fingers might feel a bit counter-intuitive to begin with, especially since you're no long leading with the thumb.

Now, just to keep you on your toes, try playing it in 6/8 (*right*). It's the self-same pattern but with the accents in a different place than they appear in 3/4.

Reminiscent of the strumming exercise at the bottom of page 65, this will help develop a sense of independence in the fingers— especially if you try switching between 6/8 and 3/4 every few bars.

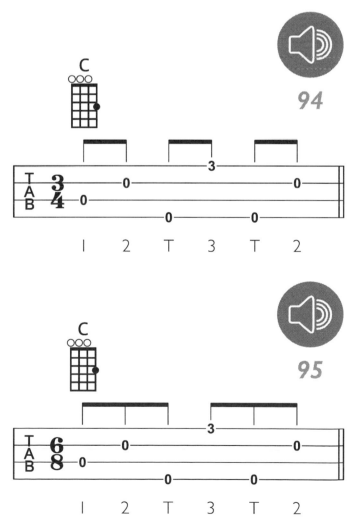

Yesterday

The Beatles

Perhaps it was fitting that such a successful song as 'Yesterday' should have its fair share of conflicting anecdotes. Most people agree it was a McCartney solo effort that took him a long time to complete and had to wait even longer for a release since it did not fit in with The Beatles' output at the time. Its stopgap title was 'Scrambled Eggs' until the lyric was completed. None of it mattered much since over the past 50 years or so its success has been truly phenomenal.

In 'Yesterday', chords mostly change once or twice per bar, so you've got time to play the two-beat pattern at least once through on each chord.

In the chorus, though, there's a bar with four chords— Dm-C-B♭-Dm—at a rate of one per beat.

Picking in this bar is tricky, so the most effective way to handle these chords is to strum once on each one, as shown by the wiggly arrows.

The two chords at the very end, lasting two beats each, should be treated the same way.

Fingerpicking

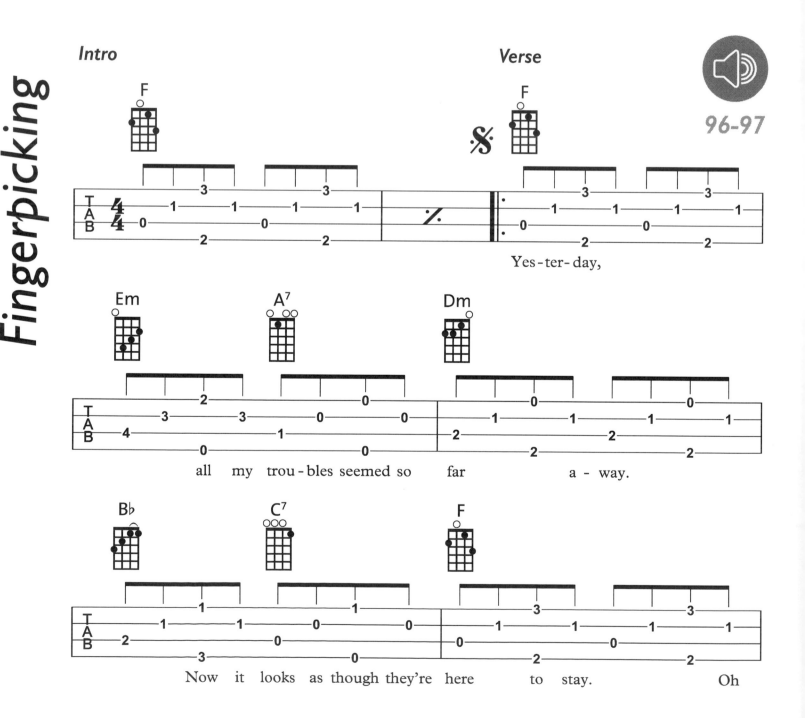

96-97

Full chords and lyrics for this song can be found at the back of the book

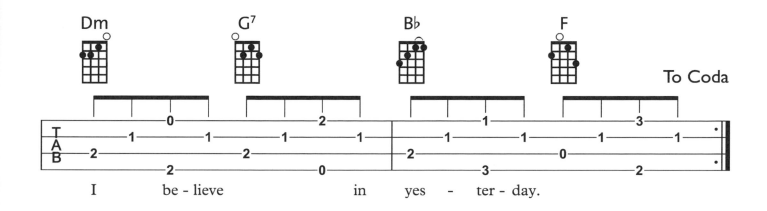

I be-lieve in yes - ter - day.

To Coda

Chorus

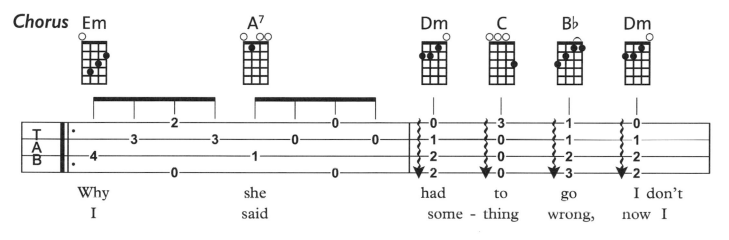

Why she had to go I don't
I said some - thing wrong, now I

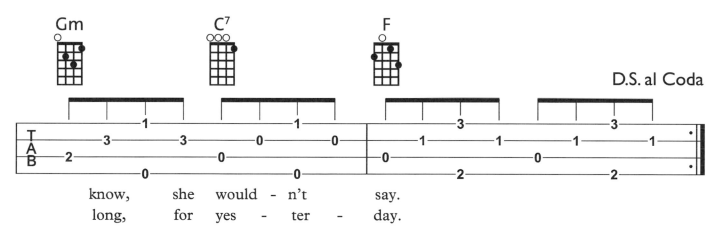

D.S. al Coda

know, she would - n't say.
long, for yes - ter - day.

Coda

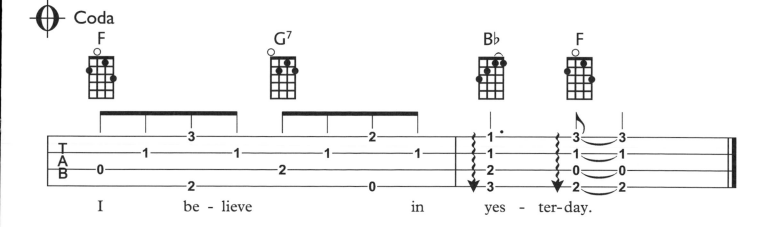

I be - lieve in yes - ter-day.

Fingerpicking

Don't Think Twice, It's All Right

Bob Dylan

Perhaps the iconic song from an iconic album, 'Don't Think Twice, It's All Right' was written by Bob Dylan while his girlfriend of the day was showing reluctance to come back from a trip to Italy. The sleeve of the album, *The Freewheelin' Bob Dylan*, featured the young folk singer, collar up to the cold New York City weather, with Suze Rotolo on his arm. He was close to the end of a relationship but right at the start of an extraordinary career.

For a faster fingerpicking in a bluegrass or up-tempo country style, you'll need a solid technique.

Here's a suitable pattern, firstly in a one-bar form:

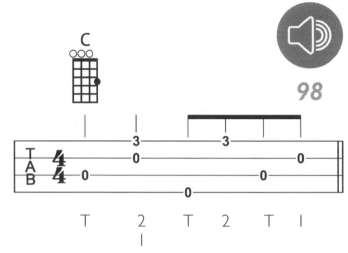

As a warm-up for the song, try playing this sequence a few times (*below*). It's the first four bars of the intro, and it crops up elsewhere as well.

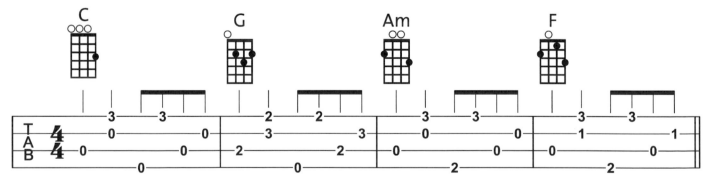

If you can play this passage smoothly, you'll be in good shape to tackle the song. Try changing to any old chord, as long as you keep the picking pattern going smoothly.

Finger Independence

Moving to random chords while you keep a picking pattern going can be a good way to get independence in the fingers, since you force yourself to stop concentrating on the right hand while you worry about what the left hand is doing!

Rolling the pattern

At higher speeds, where a single chord continues for another bar, you could keep the pattern 'rolling' like this:

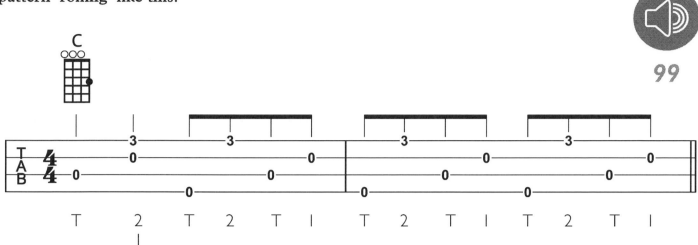

The rolling variation is essentially the same as the very first pattern we looked at (page 78), but shifted by a beat.

As always, start slowly, and build up the tempo gradually until it becomes almost intuitive.

What really brings this picking pattern to life, though, is placing accents on the **off-beats**—the '*ands*'. Here's exactly the same thing, but this time with accents on the second of each pair of eighth-notes.

This can create an effective *syncopation*—a rhythmic displacement of accents that's popular in ragtime and jazz, for instance. Try to let the accented notes ring on (and loudly).

It'll take a while to master the subtleties, but this kind of pattern is great fun to play fast and it's exciting to hear it done well.

In the above pattern, the accented off-beats are always on the top two strings. If you exaggerate the effect at a suitably fast tempo, you'll find you're almost tugging at those two strings to create the sound you're after.

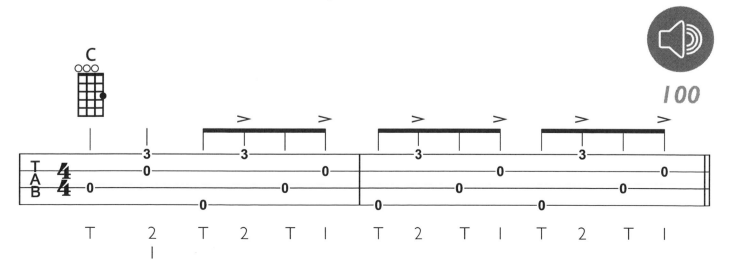

Don't Think Twice, It's All Right

Bob Dylan

Fingerpicking

Intro

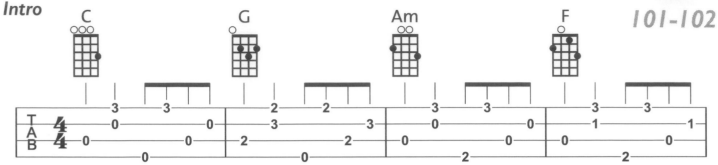

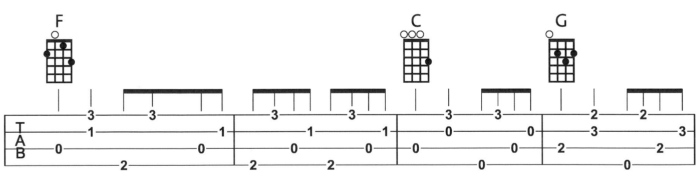

Verse

It

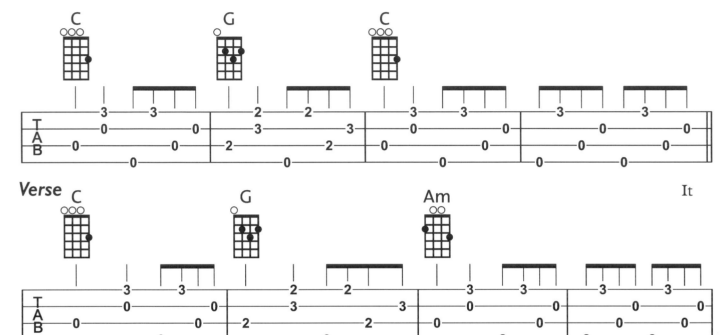

ain't no   use   to   sit and   won-der why,   babe,

it don't mat-ter   an-y - how.   An' it

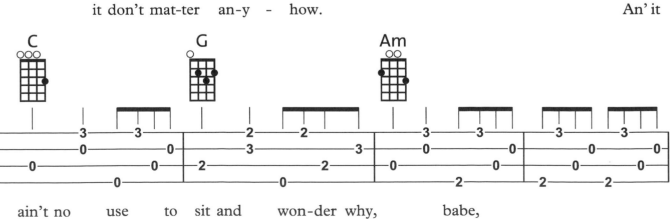

ain't no   use   to   sit and   won-der why,   babe,

*Full chords and lyrics for this song can
be found at the back of the book*

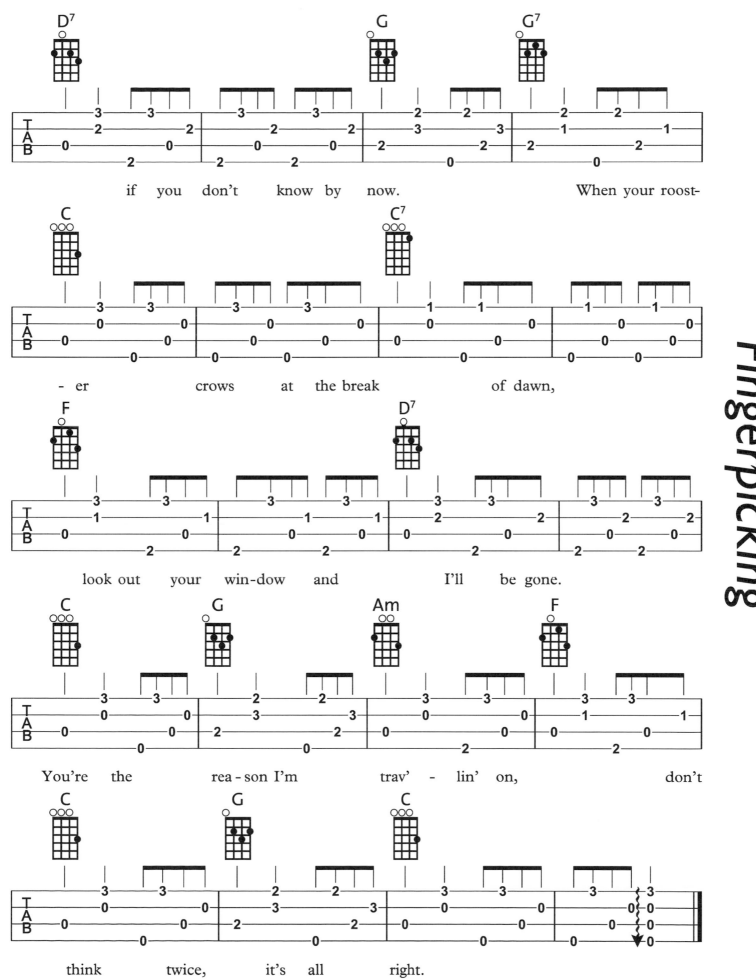

Palm Muting

Damping with the right hand

Now for a technique that will help you create a more percussive strumming style. The **chuck** (also called the **chunk**) is a heavy, solid down-strum designed to provide a strong accent within a strumming pattern.

Strum down as normal, but let your hand carry through until the heel of the palm comes to rest on the strings. This immediately mutes the strings, cutting the chord dead.

If you do this with enough energy, you'll make a loud, percussive sound that contrasts with the standard strumming.

Typically it's played on beats 2 and 4, emulating a snare drum.

Practise making the chuck—then strumming back up afterwards. It's important to be able to integrate it into a standard down-up strumming move.

A percussive sound like a chuck is often written as an 'x', like so (*right*):

103

(Sittin' On) The Dock Of The Bay
Otis Redding

It was to be Otis Redding's last recording but '(Sittin' On) The Dock Of The Bay' would have been special without its unbidden aura of farewell. Redding wrote it in Sausalito just across the bay from San Francisco not long after his triumph at the Monterey Pop Festival. He had ambitions to move into new musical territory and try a lighter feel than that of some of his grittier soul numbers. It was recorded in December shortly before Redding's death in a plane crash.

Once you've got used to the chuck, try playing a continuous down-up strum in eighths, with a chuck on the 2nd and 4th beat (*right*).

This song is ideal for practising this rhythm. Once you've got the hang of it, you'll find you return to this rhythm again and again.

104

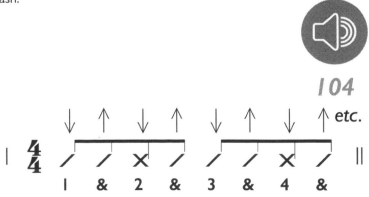

Full chords and lyrics for this song can be found at the back of the book

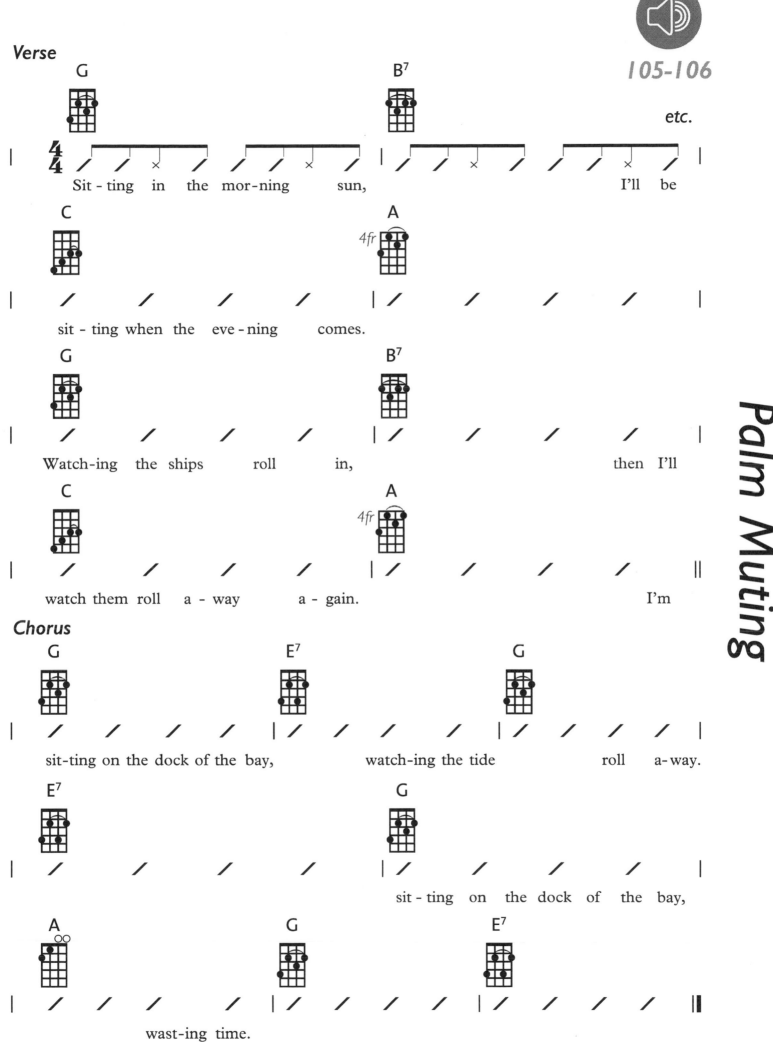

Palm Muting

89

More palm muting

Palm muting can be used to create a different percussive sound by simply bringing the strumming hand down onto the strings *without actually strumming*. The impact of the palm will create a sharp click as the strings are slapped against the fingerboard.

This useful technique doesn't really have a name, but perhaps we can call it a **ghost strum**, and notate it with a smaller 'x' note head.

Try playing the 'Dock Of The Bay' pattern again, and replace the chuck with a subtler ghost strum. Experiment with the force, angle and hand shape until you get a pleasing 'tick'.

For 'I Shot The Sheriff', the suggested strumming pattern combines these ghost strums with 'proper' ones.

Start by making sure the strumming hand is moving in constant sixteenths, then focus on the pairs of genuine strums that are played on '1 &' and '3 &'. Now add the chucks on '2 &' and '4 &', and finally fill out the rest of the pattern with little dabs onto the strings—our so-called *ghost* strums.

The result is a dynamic rhythm that with a bit of practice will sound very full and impressive.

Notice that each *ghost* down-strum is accompanied by a *ghost* up-strum. In theory, nothing actually happens here, but in practice you'll probably find that the strumming hand rubs lightly against the strings as it moves off them and a ghosted sound is heard.

107

Gm

I Shot The Sheriff

Bob Marley

Bob Marley's confrontational song was taken from The Wailers' album *Burnin'* and released as a 12″ single that enjoyed some international chart success. The song would soon reach a wider audience still when Eric Clapton covered it the following year on his *461 Ocean Boulevard* album.

Play the above pattern all the way through for this song, concentrating on a steady, unhurried beat.

As you can see, the instrumental riff at the end of each verse is included here in tab form. It starts high on the 10th fret. You'll probably find it easiest to fret the pairs of notes on each string with the third and first fingers.

> This arrangement is the same as the Eric Clapton version, which goes at quite a fast tempo, but the original Bob Marley version uses the same chords.

One last thing—a fancy chord name, E♭9. It's actually a variant on E♭7, but with the 9th note of the scale (F) added.

Full chords and lyrics for this song can be found at the back of the book

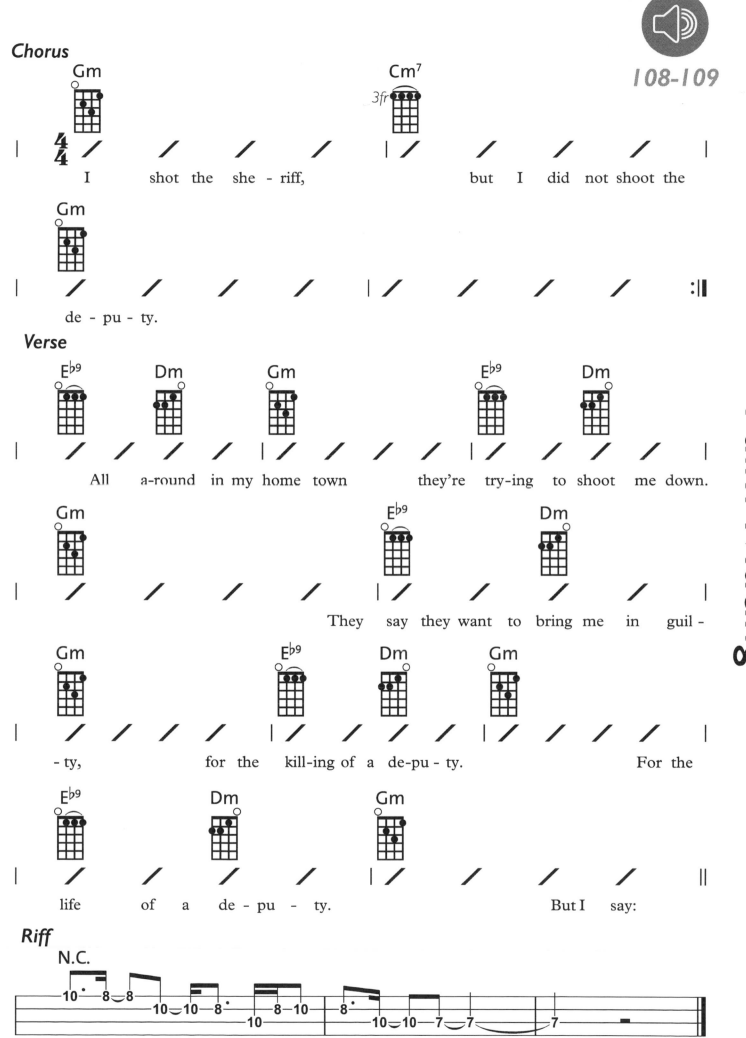

Chorus

Gm   Cm⁷

I   shot   the   she - riff,   but   I   did   not shoot the

Gm

de - pu - ty.

Verse

E♭9   Dm   Gm   E♭9   Dm

All   a-round   in my home town   they're   try-ing   to shoot   me down.

Gm   E♭9   Dm

They   say they want   to   bring me   in   guil -

Gm   E♭9   Dm   Gm

- ty,   for   the   kill-ing of a de-pu - ty.   For the

E♭9   Dm   Gm

life   of   a   de - pu - ty.   But I   say:

Riff

N.C.

Palm Muting

Let's look at another very popular use of palm muting, often used to give songs a laid-back jazz feel.

Before we look at the technique, though, we'll need to study the rhythm.

Swung eighth-notes

Up till now, whenever the beat is split into two, making eighth-notes, we've taken it for granted that the split is even, meaning that '&' happens exactly halfway through the beat:

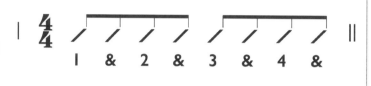

In jazz styles, though, the split is uneven. The '&' is placed more than halfway through the beat. Effectively this means that the first half of the beat lasts longer. It's still written the same way but is often marked **swing**.

You could think of it this way: imagine eighth-note triplets, with the first two joined together (*below*). This would mean that the first 'half' of the beat is twice as long as the second 'half'.

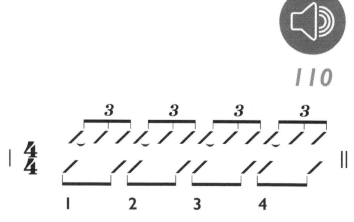

> To get a feel for these swung eighths, be sure to listen to the audio example, comparing them to 'straight' eighth-notes.

So, let's play a simple *swung* eighth-note pattern. On the beat, we'll play a solid chuck, bringing the hand down onto the strings; then off the beat, a standard up-strum.

The main difference between the down-strum and up-strum in this pattern is that the down-strum is immediately muted with the palm, while the up-strum is allowed to ring on for its entire duration:

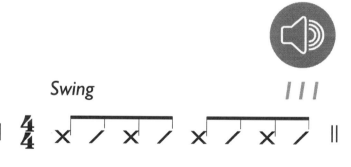

Don't forget, the up-strums are played later than usual, since they're swung eighth-notes. Check the audio example to hear the subtle swing effect.

Let's put this rhythm into practice with a standard jazz-style chord sequence (*opposite*). Take it at an easy, lazy, tempo, and exaggerate the swing. You'll find that if you increase the speed, the difference in duration between the first and second eighths naturally decreases.

Swing Exercise

Swing

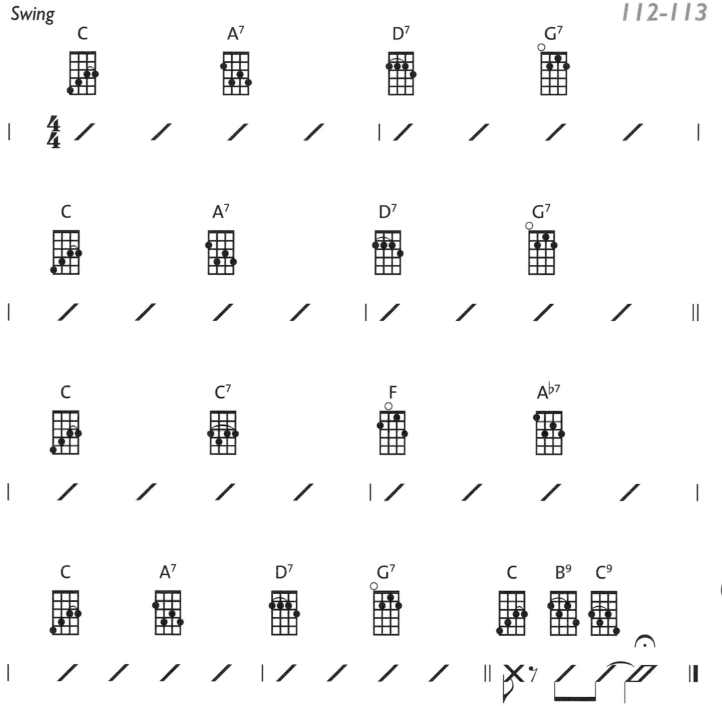

Palm Muting

In the final bar, play a single chuck, as usual, on the first beat; but then don't play a following up-strum—this is notated with the eighth-note rest. Finally play the two shapes shown, B⁹ and C⁹, on consecutive eighths, allowing the last chord to ring on.

The ⌢ symbol placed over the final chord, is called a *fermata*, or *pause*. It indicates that the music is held on for longer than the duration shown.

By the way, 'Crazy' (page 62) should be played with a gentle swing feel. Go back and play it through again, and you'll see how swung eighths add to the character of the song.

Alternatively, play it in 12/8—with proper triplets for each beat—for a more driven, dynamic feel.

Formby-Style Split Stroke
Creating that authentic sound

When we first looked at the split stroke (page 66) we used it to play *triplet eighth-notes*—three strums in the space of a single beat.

To finish off, let's have a bit of fun with an iconic strumming style that is inextricably associated with George Formby. To begin with, go back to page 66 and familiarise yourself with the *alternative* method of playing the split stroke, which only uses the index finger.

Formby's strumming style featured consecutive split strokes played in standard eighth-notes. By grouping eighth-notes in this way, it's easy to create some unusual *syncopated* accents.

Here's a bar of eighth-notes in 4/4, with two lots of split strokes. Each split stroke occupies three eighth-notes, starting with a full down-strum (full arrow) and followed by a short up-strum and a short down-strum (small arrow heads).

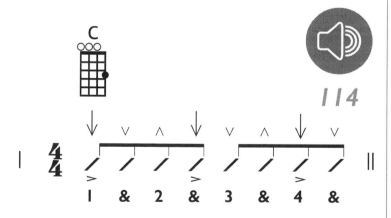

This leaves just two eighth-notes to finish the bar, which is achieved by playing the first two strums of a new split stroke.

The full strum at the start of each split stroke creates a strong accent compared to the other, smaller strums. You could think of it as "cof-fee cup, cof-fee cup, cof-fee" to get a feel for the accents. At speed this can sound quite exciting.

Take a listen to the audio example and pay attention to the placement of the accents. It's played slowly at first, and then up to speed.

Adding details
Once you've got the hang of that, it's time to take it up a notch. On a simple C chord, strum as normal at the start of each split stroke. In the in-between strums lift the finger off the chord leaving the top string open. This slight change of chord emphasises the accents, which is exactly what George Formby typically did.

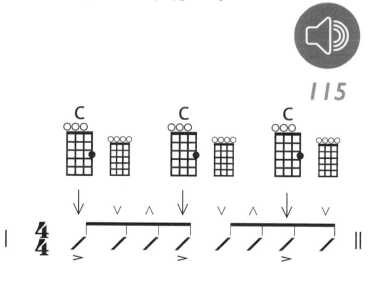

In fact almost any chord that is fingered on the top string is suitable for this kind of thing. Try it on G7 too:

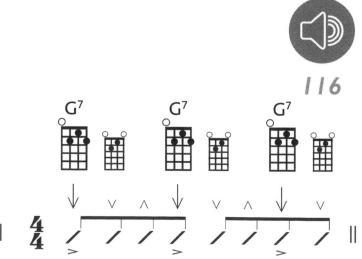

Formby-Style Exercise

Try putting this new technique into practice with a typical Formby-style chord sequence. For the chords of C, G⁷, C⁷ and F, play the full strums with the complete chord shape, but lift the finger off the top string for the in-between strums. Harmonically, this doesn't work so well for the A♭7 chord, as the open top string clashes, but it'll work fine everywhere else.

Finally, notice the bracketed group of three eighth-notes towards the end: a **triplet** played in the space of two beats.

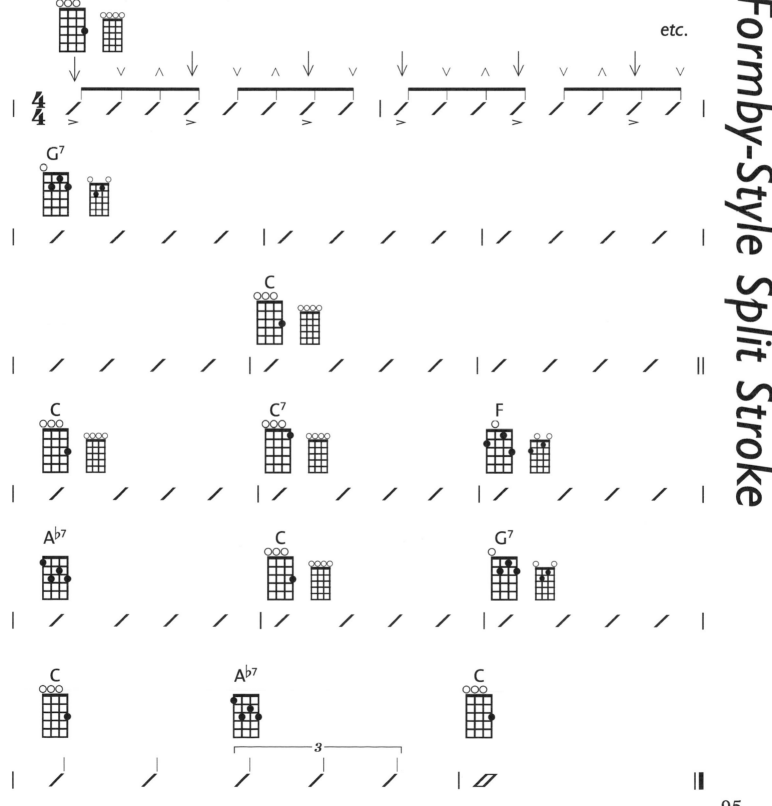

Formby-Style Split Stroke

95

Even More Chords

Almost every other shape you'll need...

We've played major chords, minor chords, chords with sevenths, and even a couple of ninths.

Although some of the more esoteric jazz shapes are beyond the scope of this book, we should take a look at some of the more common chord types you'll come across.

Major seventh

The **seventh** chords we saw on page 56 have a built-in dissonance that makes them perfect for creating tension-and-release movement in chord progressions.

There's another kind of seventh, the so-called **major seventh** (maj⁷), that has a quite different role. You might describe the sound of a major seventh chord as 'floaty'.

The maj⁷ is used most often instead of a standard major chord to add colour. In the diagrams below, each major shape has been altered by a single fret to create the equivalent major seventh shape. Of course, these new shapes can also be used as the basis for barre chords, too.

To get a feel for the way they sound, try returning to 'Crazy' (page 62) and play Cmaj⁷ instead of the straight C chords.

'Crazy' is the kind of song that can handle the more sophisticated sound of maj⁷ chords. You'll often hear maj⁷ chords in jazz and bossa nova, for example, but it might sound a bit out of place in straight-ahead rock and pop.

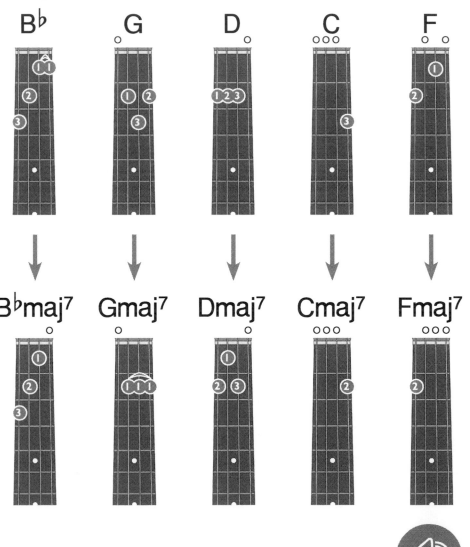

119-123

96

Minor seventh

The **minor seventh** (m^7) is a variation on the standard minor chords we've played.

The extra note adds a warmth and complexity to simple minor chords. In fact we already played a Cm^7 chord in 'I Shot The Sheriff' (page 90). Let's look at some more m^7 shapes now.

There are five main m^7 shapes that work well on the ukulele, including a single barre across all four strings.

This is the one that we played in 'I Shot The Sheriff', barred then on the 3rd fret from Cm^7 and shown here on the 2nd fret for Bm^7.

Naturally, the two shapes shown here using open strings (Gm^7 and Em^7) can both be played as barred shapes higher up the neck.

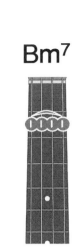

Dm⁷ B♭m⁷ Gm⁷ Bm⁷ Em⁷

124-128

Augmented

This fun chord comes in two flavours: *with a seventh* (^{7}aug) or *without* (aug). The ^{7}aug chord can replace a dominant-type chord in jazz styles and has a very distinct character.

You might see an aug chord written as $^{\#}5$ or + instead of aug—but it's the same thing. Likewise, ^{7}aug chords are often written $^{7\#5}$ or $^7+$, but they're just alternative names.

Without a seventh, the augmented chord has the peculiar characteristic that all the notes in the chord are—in theory, at least—separated from each other by two tones.

What this means in practice is that any augmented shape can be used to represent a total of three augmented chords. The B♭aug shape, shown here, could also be used for Daug or F♯aug. Baug could be D♯aug or Gaug; Caug could also be Eaug or G♯aug; and C♯aug could be Faug or Aaug as well.

129-132

B♭aug C♯aug B♭⁷aug C♯⁷aug

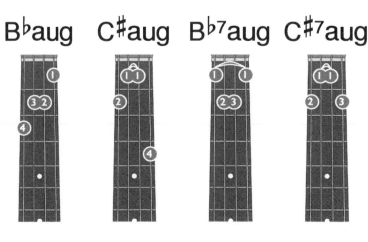

97

Diminished

We encountered a single *diminished* chord in 'Crazy' (page 62). The shape we saw there is really the only one you need to play diminished chords on the uke.

Diminished chords have a very special characteristic—they consist of four notes, all equidistant. This means that in any position the shape can represent four different chords, as shown below.

C#dim

Cdim = E♭dim = F#dim = Adim

C#dim = Edim = Gdim = B♭dim

Ddim = Fdim = A♭dim = Bdim

Diminished chords commonly occur in musical hall songs, in jazz and bossa nova, in show tunes and novelty songs. The very distinctive flavour of a diminished chord can transform the overall 'feel' of any song it's used in.

Typically, diminished chords are used as a replacement for a dominant-type chord, and are played *a semitone higher* than the chord they replace. For example, try using A♭dim instead of G^7, or Fdim instead of E^7. A little goes a long way with these kinds of chords, and it's easy to overdo it, so use them sparingly!

You could try playing Blueberry Hill or Crazy again, replacing any ^{7} chord with a dim chord a semitone higher. You'll get some odd results, but it'll give you a good idea of the diminished sound!

Exercise For New Chord Types

To finish up, let's put some of these chord types to good use in a little exercise designed to give you a feel for their sound.

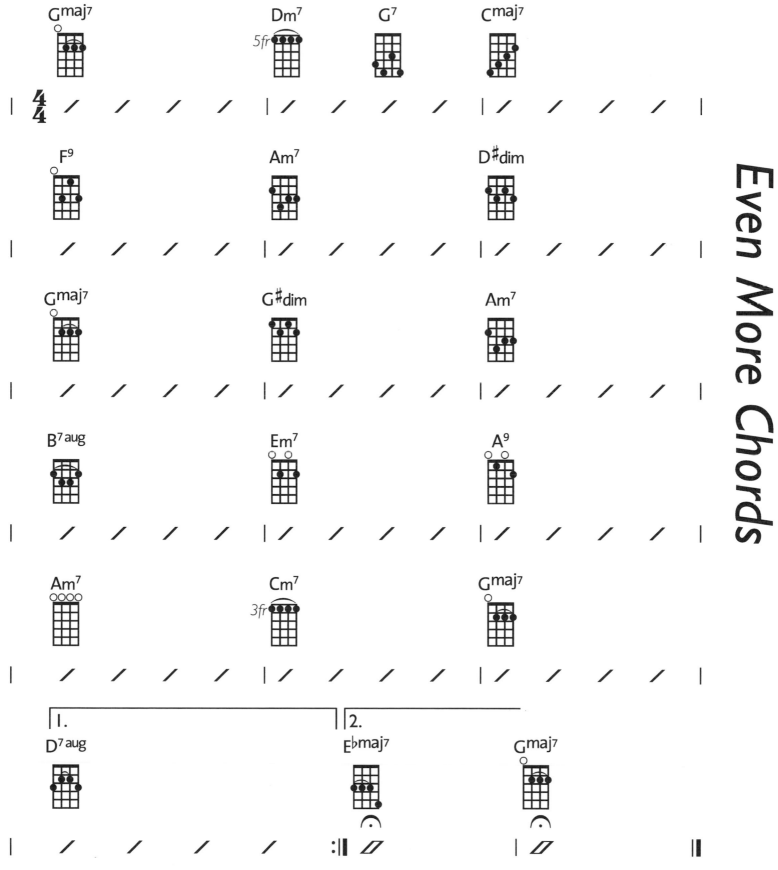

Even More Chords

99

Blowin' In The Wind *(page 20)*

Verse 1

C   F   G⁷   C

How many roads must a man walk down,

           F   C

Before you call him a man?

              F   G⁷

Yes, 'n' how many seas must the white dove

C

sail?

           F   G⁷

Before she sleeps in the sand?

       C   F   G⁷

Yes, 'n' how many times must the cannon-

      C

balls fly,

         F   C

Before they're forever banned?

Chorus

      F   G⁷   C

The answer, my friend, is blowin' in the wind,

      F   G⁷   C

The answer is blowin' in the wind.

Verse 2

How many years can a mountain exist
Before it's washed to the sea?
Yes, 'n' how many years can some people exist
Before they're allowed to be free?
Yes, 'n' how many times can a man turn his head
Pretending he just doesn't see?

Verse 3

How many times must a man look up
Before he can see the sky?
Yes, 'n' how many ears must one man have
Before he can hear people cry?
Yes, 'n' how many deaths will it take till he knows
That too many people have died?
The answer, my friend, is blowin' in the wind
The answer is blowin' in the wind.

Love Me Do *(page 22)*

Verse 1

G   C   G   C

Love, love me do, you know I love you,

       G   C   N. C.

I'll always be true, so please

             G   C   G

Love me do.

Bridge

D   C   G

Someone to love, somebody new,

D   C   G

Someone to love, someone like you.

Verse 2

Love, love me do, you know I love you,
I'll always be true, so please
Love me do. Oh, love me do.

Songbook

Redemption Song *(page 24)*

Verse 1

    G   Em

Oh, pirates, yes, they rob I.

C   Am

Sold I to the merchant ships

G   Em

Minutes after they took I

C   Am

From the bottomless pit.

    G   Em

But my hand was made strong

    C   Am

By the hand of the Almighty.

    G   Em

We forward in this generation

C   Am

Triumphantly.

Chorus

             G

Won't you help to sing

C   D   G   C   D

These songs of freedom?

      Em   C   D

'Cause all I ever had,

C   D   G

  Redemption songs,

C   D   G

  Redemption songs.

Verse 2

Emancipate yourselves from mental slav'ry,
None but ourselves can free our minds.
Have no fear for atomic energy,
'Cause none of them can stop the time.
How long shall they kill our prophets,
While we stand aside and look?
Some say it's just a part of it.
We've got to fulfil the book.

Stand By Me *(page 32)*

Verse 1

          G

When the night has come,

Em

    And the land is dark,

          C D^7 G

And the moon is the only light we'll see.

                      Em

No I won't be afraid, oh I won't be afraid

          C D^7 G

Just as long as you stand, stand by me.

Chorus

                  G

So darling, darling stand by me,

    Em

Oh stand by me.

      C D^7

Oh stand, stand by me,

G

Stand by me.

Verse 2

If the sky that we look upon,
Should tumble and fall
Or the mountains should crumble to the sea.
I won't cry, I won't cry, no I won't shed a tear
Just as long as you stand, stand by me.

Brown Eyed Girl *(page 34)*

Words & Music by Van Morrison
© Copyright 1967 Web IV Music Inc.
Universal Music Publishing Limited.
All Rights Reserved. International Copyright Secured.

Verse 1

G   C
Hey, where did we go?
G   D
Days when the rains came?
G   C
Down in the hollow
G   D
Playing a new game,
G   C
Laughing and a-running, hey, hey,
G   D
Skipping and a-jumping
G   C
In the misty morning fog with
G   D
Our, our hearts a-thumping
       C   D   G   Em
And you, my brown eyed girl,
C   D   G
You, my brown eyed girl.

Verse 2

Whatever happened
To Tuesday and so slow?
Going down to the old mine with a
Transistor radio.
Standing in the sunlight laughing
Hidin' b'hind a rainbow's wall,
Slipping and a-sliding
All along the waterfall
With you, my brown eyed girl,
You, my brown eyed girl.

Chorus

D
Do you remember when we used to sing
G   C   G   D
Sha la la la la la la la la la la la di da?
G   C   G   D
Sha la la la la la la la la la la la di dah
G
La di da.

Verse 3

So hard to find my way
Now that I'm all on my own.
I saw you just the other day,
My, how you have grown!
Cast my memory back there, Lord,
Sometime I'm overcome thinking about
Making love in the green grass
Behind the stadium
With you, my brown eyed girl,
You, my brown eyed girl.

Songbook

Mull Of Kintyre *(page 42)*

Chorus

D   G   D
Mull of Kintyre, oh mist rolling in from the sea,
      G
My desire is always to be here,
  D
Oh Mull of Kintyre.

Verse 1

D
Far have I travelled and much have I seen.
G   D
Dark distant mountains with valleys of green.
Past painted deserts, the sunset's on fire
      G   A   D
As he carries me home to the Mull of Kintyre.

Verse 2

Sweep through the heather,
Like deer in the glen.
Carry me back to the days I knew then.
Nights when we sang like a heavenly choir,
Of the life and the times of the Mull of
Kintyre.

Verse 3

Smiles in the sunshine and tears in the rain
Still take me back where my memories
remain,
Flickering embers grow higher and higher as
They carry me back to the Mull of Kintyre.

Ain't No Sunshine *(page 46)*

Verse 1

                         Am   Em G
Ain't no sunshine when she's gone.
Am   Em G
  It's not warm when she's away.
Am   Em
   Ain't no sunshine when she's gone,
           Dm
And she's always gone too long,
          Am Em G Am
Any time she goes away.

Verse 2

Wonder this time where she's gone.
Wonder if she's gone to stay.
Ain't no sunshine when she's gone,
And this house just ain't no home,
Any time she goes away.

Verse 3

And I know, I know, I know…
Hey, I oughta leave the young thing alone,
But ain't no sunshine when she's gone.

Verse 4

Ain't no sunshine when she's gone,
Only darkness every day.
Ain't no sunshine when she's gone,
And this house just ain't no home,
Any time she goes away.

Outro

Any time she goes away,
Any time she goes away,
Any time she goes away.

Songbook

Hey, Soul Sister *(page 50)*

Words & Music by Espen Lind, Pat Monahan & Amund Bjørklund
© Copyright 2009 EMI April Music Inc., Blue Lamp Music and Stellar Songs Ltd.
All Rights for Blue Lamp Music Controlled and Administered by EMI April Music Inc.
All Rights for Stellar Songs Ltd in the U.S. and Canada Controlled and Administered by EMI Blackwood Music Inc.
All Rights Reserved. International Copyright Secured.

Songbook

Intro

E   B   C♯m   A
   Hey,   hey,   hey.

Verse 1

   E
Your lipstick stains
B   C♯m
  On the front lobe of my left side brains
A   E
   I knew I wouldn't forget you and so I went
   B   C♯m A B
And let you blow my mind.
   E
Your sweet moonbeam,
B
   The smell of you in ev'ry
C♯m
Single dream I dream.
A   E
   I knew when we collided
           B
You're the one I have decided
         C♯m A B
Who's one of my kind.

Chorus

A   B
Hey soul sister, ain't that Mr. Mister
     A
On the radio, stereo?
     B
The way you move ain't fair, you know.
   A   B
Hey,   soul sister, I don't wanna miss
   A   B
A single thing you do tonight.
E   B   C♯m   A
   Hey,   hey,   hey.

Verse 2

Just in time, I'm so glad you have
A one track mind like me.
You gave my life direction,
A game show love connection we can't deny.
I'm so obsessed,
My heart is bound to beat
Right out my untrimmed chest.
I believe in you, like a virgin, you're Madonna.
And I'm always gonna wanna blow your mind.

Verse 3

E
The way you can cut a rug,
B   C♯m
   Watching you is the only drug I need.
You're so gangster, I'm so thug,
          A
You're the only one I'm dreaming of.
        E   B
You see, I can be myself now finally,
                  C♯m
In fact there's nothing I can't be.
                A   B
I want the world to see you'll be with me.

104

Walk On The Wild Side *(page 54)*

Verse 1

C   F
Holly came from Miami F.L.A.,
C   F
Hitch-hiked her way across the U.S.A.,
C   Dm
Plucked her eyebrows on the way,
F   Dm
Shaved her legs and then he was a she,

Chorus

She says,
 C   F
"Hcy, babe, take a walk on the wild side."
I said,
C   F
"Hey honey, take a walk on the wild side."

Verse 2

Little Joe never once gave it away,
Everybody had to pay and pay,
A hustle here and a hustle there,
New York City is the place where they said:

Verse 3

Sugar Plum Fairy came and hit the streets,
Lookin' for soul food and a place to eat,
Went to the Apollo
You should have seen him go, go, go.

Verse 4

Jackie is just speeding away,
Thought she was James Dean for a day,
Then I guess she had to crash,
Valium would have helped that bash.

Jambalaya (On The Bayou) *(page 57)*

Verse 1

                C   G⁷
Goodbye Joe, me gotta go, me oh my-oh.
                               C
Me gotta go, pole the pirogue down the bayou.
                        G^7
My Yvonne, sweetest one, me oh my-oh.
                              C
Son of a gun we'll have big fun on the bayou.

Chorus

Jambalay', crawfish pie, and file gumbo.
For tonight I'm gonna see my cher a-mie-oh.
Pick guitar, fill fruit jar, and be gay-oh.
Son of a gun we'll have big fun on the bayou.

Verse 2

Thibodaux, Fontaineaux, the place is buzzin'.
Kinfolk come to see Yvonne by the dozen.
Dress in style and go hog-wild, me oh my-oh.
Son of a gun we'll have big fun on the bayou.

Songbook

Crazy *(page 62)*

Verse 1

C   A⁷   Dm
Crazy, crazy for feeling so lonely.
  G⁷   C C#dim Dm G⁷
I'm crazy, crazy for feeling so blue.

Verse 2

I knew, you'd love me as long as you wanted,
And then someday,
                   C F C C⁷
You'd leave me for somebody new.

Chorus

F   C
Worry, why do I let myself worry?
D⁷   G⁷
Wond'ring what in the world did I do?

Verse 3

Crazy,
For thinking that my love could hold you.
  F   Em   Dm
I'm crazy for trying and crazy
    A⁷
For crying
   Dm   G⁷ C   F   C
And crazy for loving you.

Norwegian Wood (This Bird Has Flown) *(page 68)*

Intro

E   D A   E

Verse 1

E
I once had a girl,
               D A   E
Or should I say she once had me.
E
She showed me her room, isn't it good.
D   A E
Norwegian Wood.

Chorus 1

    Em
She asked me to stay
                      A
And she told me to sit anywhere.
    Em
So I looked around and I noticed
            F#m   B
There wasn't a chair.

Verse 2

I sat on a rug, biding my time,
Drinking her wine.
We talked until two, and then she said,
"It's time for bed."

Chorus 2

She told me she worked in the morning
And started to laugh,
I told her I didn't and crawled off
To sleep in the bath.

Verse 3

And when I awoke I was alone,
This bird had flown.
So I lit a fire, isn't it good.
Norwegian Wood.

Songbook

Blueberry Hill (page 70)

Verse 1

$\qquad$ E $\qquad$ B

I found my thrill, on Blueberry Hill,

$\qquad$ F#7 $\qquad$ B E B

On Blueberry Hill, when I found you.

Verse 2

The moon stood still, on Blueberry Hill,

And lingered until,

$\qquad$ B $\quad$ Em $\quad$ B

My dream came true.

Chorus

$\quad$ F#7 $\qquad$ B

The wind in the willows played

$\quad$ F#7 $\qquad$ B

Love's sweet melody,

$\quad$ A#7 $\qquad$ D#m $\qquad$ A#7 $\quad$ D#m

But all of those vows you made

$\quad$ A#7 $\quad$ D#7 $\quad$ F#7

Are never to be.

Verse 3

Though we're apart, you're part of me still,

For you were my thrill, on Blueberry Hill.

Yesterday (page 82)

Verse 1

F $\qquad$ Em $\qquad$ A7

Yesterday, $\quad$ all my troubles seemed so

Dm

Far away.

B♭ $\qquad$ C7 $\qquad$ F

$\quad$ Now it looks as though they're here to stay.

$\quad$ Dm $\quad$ G7 $\quad$ B♭ $\quad$ F

Oh, I believe in yesterday.

Verse 2

Suddenly, I'm not half the man I used to be.

There's a shadow hanging over me.

Oh, yesterday came suddenly.

Bridge

Em $\quad$ A7 $\quad$ Dm $\quad$ C $\quad$ B♭ $\quad$ Dm $\qquad$ Gm

Why she had to go I don't know,

$\qquad$ C7 $\qquad$ F

She wouldn't say.

Em $\quad$ A7 $\quad$ Dm $\quad$ C $\qquad$ B♭ $\qquad$ Dm $\quad$ Gm

I $\quad$ said something wrong now I long

$\qquad$ C7 $\quad$ F

For yesterday.

Verse 3 & 4

Yesterday, love was such an easy game to play.

Now I need a place to hide away.

Oh, I believe in yesterday.

Songbook

Don't Think Twice, It's All Right

(page 86)

Words & Music by Bob Dylan
Copyright © 1963 Warner Bros. Inc.
Copyright © Renewed 1991 Special Rider Music.
All Rights Reserved. International Copyright Secured.

Intro

C   G   Am   F   C   G   C

Verse 1

C   G   Am
It ain't no use to sit and wonder why, babe
F   C   G
  It don't matter, anyhow
      C   G   Am
An' it ain't no use to sit and wonder why, babe
D⁷   G   G⁷
  If you don't know by now
          C   C⁷
When your rooster crows at the break of dawn
  F   D⁷
  Look out your window and I'll be gone
C   G   Am   F
You're the reason I'm trav'lin' on
      C   G   C
Don't think twice, it's all right

Verse 2

It ain't no use in turnin' on your light, babe
That light I never knowed
An' it ain't no use in turnin' on your light, babe
I'm on the dark side of the road
Still I wish there was somethin'
You would do or say
To try and make me change my mind and stay
We never did too much talkin' anyway
So don't think twice, it's all right

Verse 3

It ain't no use in callin' out my name, gal
Like you never did before
It ain't no use in callin' out my name, gal
I can't hear you anymore
I'm a-thinkin' and a-wond'rin'
All the way down the road
I once loved a woman, a child I'm told
I give her my heart but she wanted my soul
But don't think twice, it's all right

Verse 4

I'm walkin' down that long,
Lonesome road, babe
Where I'm bound, I can't tell
But goodbye's too good a word, gal
So I'll just say fare thee well
I ain't sayin' you treated me unkind
You could have done better but I don't mind
You just kinda wasted my precious time
But don't think twice, it's all right

Songbook

(Sittin' On) The Dock Of The Bay

(page 88)

Verse 1

G   B⁷

Sitting in the morning sun,

      C   A

I'll be sitting when the evening comes.

G   B⁷

Watching the ships roll in,

      C   A

Then I'll watch them roll away again.

Chorus

G   E⁷

I'm sitting on the dock of the bay,

                 G   E⁷

Watching the tide roll away.

G   A

Sitting on the dock of the bay,

          G   E⁷

Wasting time.

Verse 2

I left my home in Georgia,

Headed for the 'Frisco Bay.

I've had nothing to live for,

And looks like nothing's gonna come my way.

Bridge

G   D   C

Looks like nothing's gonna change.

G   D   C

Everything still remains the same.

G   D   C   G

I can't do what ten people tell me to do,

F   D

  So I guess I'll remain the same.

Verse 3

Sitting here resting my bones,

And this loneliness won't leave me alone.

Two thousand miles I roam,

Just to make this dock my home.

I Shot The Sheriff *(page 90)*

Words & Music by Bob Marley
© Copyright 1973 Fifty-Six Hope Road Music Limited/
Blackwell Fuller Music Publishing LLC.
Blue Mountain Music Limited.
All Rights Reserved. International Copyright Secured.

Chorus 1

Gm
I shot the sheriff,
Cm   Gm
But I did not shoot the deputy.
Gm
I shot the sheriff,
Cm   Gm
But I did not shoot the deputy.

Verse 1

E♭9 Dm   Gm
All around in my home town,
       E♭9   Dm   Gm
They're trying to shoot me down.
     E♭9   Dm   Gm
They say they want to bring me in guilty,
     E♭9   Dm   Gm
For the killing of a deputy.
     E♭9   Dm Gm
For the life of a deputy. But I say:

Chorus 2

I shot the sheriff,
But I swear it was in self defence.
I shot the sheriff,
And they say it is a capital offence.

Verse 2

Sheriff John Brown always hated me,
For what I don't know.
And every time that I plant a seed,
He said "Kill it, before it grows"
He said "Kill it, before it grows".

Chorus 3

I shot the sheriff,
But I swear it was in self defence.
I shot the sheriff,
And they say it is a capital offence.

Verse 3

Freedom came my way one day,
And I started out of town there.
All of a sudden I see Sheriff John Brown,
Aiming to shot me down.
So I shot, I shot him down,
And I say

Chorus 4 & 5

I shot the sheriff
But I did not shoot the deputy.
I shot the sheriff
But I did not shoot the deputy.

Verse 4

Reflexes got the better of me
And what must be must be.
Every day the bucket goes to the well
But one day the bottom will drop out,
Yes, one day the bottom will drop out.

Some Useful Chord Shapes

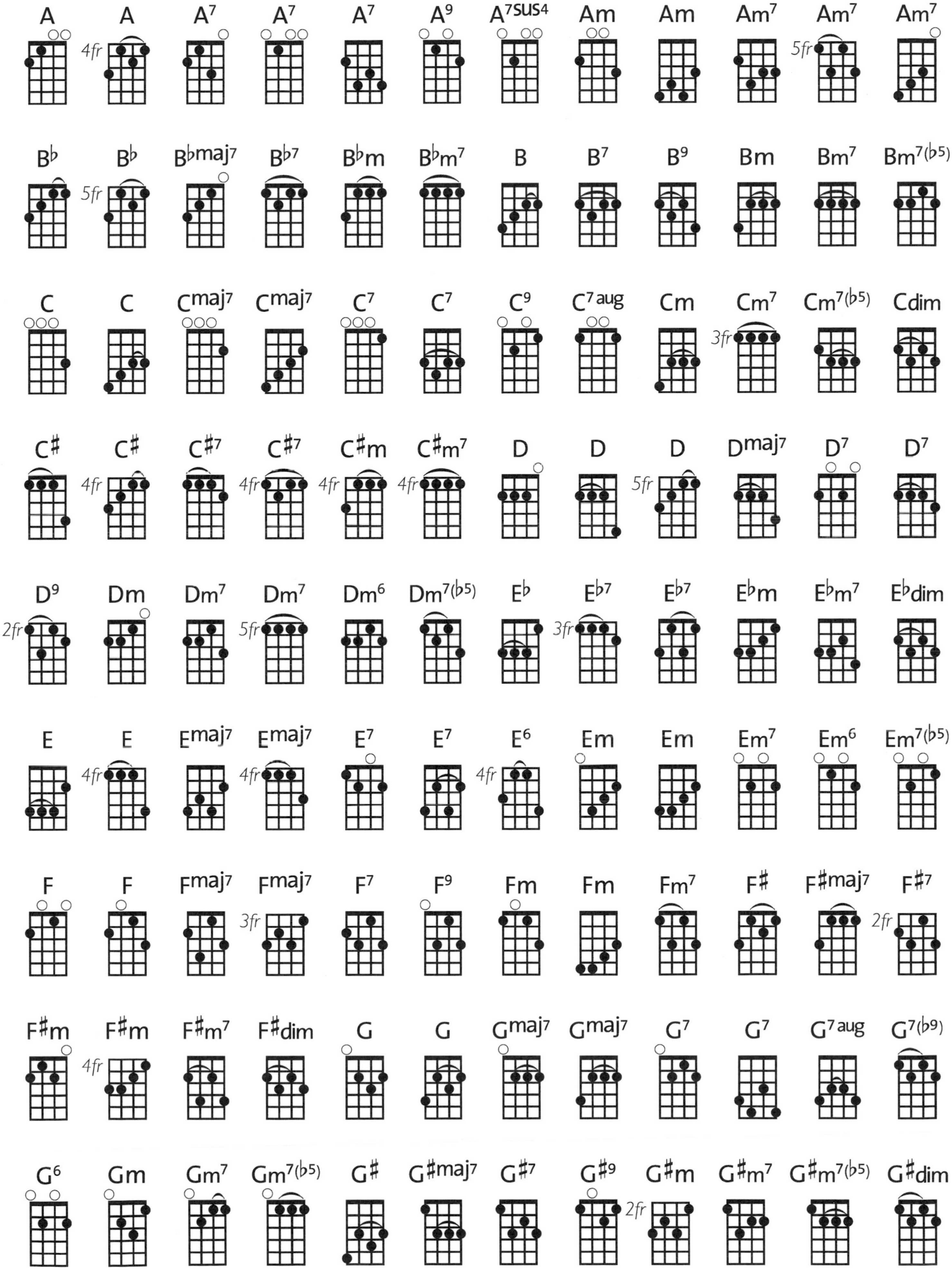
A
A
A7
A7
A7
A9
A7sus4
Am
Am
Am7
Am7
Am7
4fr
5fr
B♭
B♭
B♭maj7
B♭7
B♭m
B♭m7
B
B7
B9
Bm
Bm7
Bm7(♭5)
5fr
C
C
Cmaj7
Cmaj7
C7
C7
C9
C7 aug
Cm
Cm7
Cm7(♭5)
Cdim
3fr
C♯
C♯
C♯7
C♯7
C♯m
C♯m7
D
D
D
Dmaj7
D7
D7
4fr
4fr
4fr
4fr
5fr
D9
Dm
Dm7
Dm7
Dm6
Dm7(♭5)
E♭
E♭7
E♭7
E♭m
E♭m7
E♭dim
2fr
5fr
3fr
E
E
Emaj7
Emaj7
E7
E7
E6
Em
Em
Em7
Em6
Em7(♭5)
4fr
4fr
4fr
F
F
Fmaj7
Fmaj7
F7
F9
Fm
Fm
Fm7
F♯
F♯maj7
F♯7
3fr
2fr
F♯m
F♯m
F♯m7
F♯dim
G
G
Gmaj7
Gmaj7
G7
G7
G7 aug
G7(♭9)
4fr
G6
Gm
Gm7
Gm7(♭5)
G♯
G♯maj7
G♯7
G♯9
G♯m
G♯m7
G♯m7(♭5)
G♯dim
2fr